GROWTH

1 · GOODNESS · TRUTH · PERFECTION · CLARITY · JUSTICE · SELF CONTROL ·

2 · HELPFULNESS · ALTRUISM · LOVING · BOLD · SERVANTS HEART · DISCERNING NEEDS ·

3 · EFFICIENCY · ACTION · ENCOURAGER · ESTABLISHER · INSPIRING · EXCELLENCE ·

4 · CREATIVITY · EMPATHY · LOVE OF BEAUTY · SPACE SAVER · EMOTIONALLY HONEST ·

5 · WISDOM · VISION · STEADFASTNESS · CLARITY · FAITHFULNESS · HUMILITY ·

6 · COURAGE · GUARDIANSHIP · KINDNESS · LOYALTY · STRENGTH · FAITHFULNESS ·

7 · SPONTANEITY · JOY · THANKFULNESS · HOPE · LONG SUFFERING · VISION ·

8 · STRENGTH · ZEAL · VIGILANT · ZEALOUS · PROTECTOR · TENDERNESS ·

9 · PEACE · KINDNESS · EMPATHY · PATIENCE · GENTLENESS · UNDERSTANDING ·

WHAT PEOPLE ARE SAYING ABOUT ELISABETH BENNETT AND *THE INDIVIDUALIST: GROWING AS AN ENNEAGRAM 4*

Elisabeth has written a delightful devotional full of important information for those who want to grow in their own self-awareness and relationship with Christ. I highly recommend reading this book so you can experience transformation on a much deeper level that will bring about the change you desire in life.

—*Beth McCord*
YourEnneagramCoach.com
Author of 10 Enneagram books

I have been craving a devotional that would not only strengthen my relationship with Christ, but also authentically "get me" as an Enneagram Four. This simply knocks that out of the water. I find that, as a Four, it's hard to conform and give in to a generic devotional, and this is anything but that. It's beautifully constructed for my Four heart.

—*Audrey Bailey*
Artist, mental health advocate
Creator, Brush and Barley digital brand @brushandbarley

Elisabeth has a beautiful way of guiding the reader into a deeper understanding and self-awareness that leads to spiritual growth through the Enneagram. Through biblically sound and practical devotions, she helps you move from, "Okay, I know what type I am but what's next?" to personal, relational, and spiritual growth, so that you can live in the fullness of who you were created to be in your unique type.

—*Justin Boggs*
The Other Half Podcast
Enneagram coach, speaker, entrepreneur

Through her beautifully articulate words, Elisabeth accurately portrays the shadow side of each Enneagram type while also highlighting the rich grace and freedom found in the spiritual journey of integration. Pairing Scripture with reflection questions and prayers, the devotions help to guide the reader on the pathway of personal and spiritual growth in a powerful way that is unique to their type.

—*Meredith Boggs*
The Other Half Podcast

If you know your Enneagram type, and you're ready to make meaningful steps toward growth, this book is for you. Elisabeth combines her Enneagram expertise with her deep faith to guide readers toward self-understanding, growth, and transformation through contemplative yet practical writing. This devotional is a great tool that you'll return to again and again.

—*Steph Barron Hall*
Nine Types Co.
Enneagram writer, coach, and teacher

60-DAY
ENNEAGRAM DEVOTIONAL

the
INDIVIDUALIST

GROWING AS AN ENNEAGRAM

ELISABETH BENNETT

WHITAKER
HOUSE

Unless otherwise indicated, all Scripture quotations are taken from *The Holy Bible, English Standard Version*, © 2000, 2001, 1995 by Crossway Bibles, a division of Good News Publishers. Used by permission. All rights reserved. Scripture quotations marked (NIV) are taken from the *Holy Bible, New International Version*®, NIV®, © 1973, 1978, 1984, 2011 by Biblica, Inc.® Used by permission. All rights reserved worldwide. The "NIV" and "New International Version" are trademarks registered in the United States Patent and Trademark Office by Biblica, Inc.® Scripture quotations marked (MSG) are taken from *The Message: The Bible in Contemporary Language* by Eugene H. Peterson, © 1993, 1994, 1995, 1996, 2000, 2001, 2002. Used by permission of NavPress Publishing Group. All rights reserved. Represented by Tyndale House Publishers, Inc.

Introduction images created by Katherine Waddell.

Photo of Elisabeth Bennett by Jena Stagner of One Beautiful Life Photography.

THE INDIVIDUALIST
Growing as an Enneagram 4

www.elisabethbennettenneagram.com
Instagram: @enneagram.life
Facebook.com/enneagramlife

ISBN: 978-1-64123-509-9
eBook ISBN: 978-1-64123-510-5
Printed in the United States of America
© 2020 by Elisabeth Bennett

Whitaker House
1030 Hunt Valley Circle
New Kensington, PA 15068
www.whitakerhouse.com

Library of Congress Cataloging-in-Publication Data (Pending)

1 2 3 4 5 6 7 8 9 10 11 **LIJ** 27 26 25 24 23 22 21 20

Dedication

To every Four holding this book, you are known, loved,
and belong right where God has placed you.

Contents

Foreword...11

Acknowledgments 15

Introduction: What Is the Enneagram?....................19

What It Means to Be an Individualist........................27

All About Being a Four 31

So I'm a Four. What Now? 39

Your Guides for This Journey....................................43

10 Days of Finding Beauty in Life
    How We Reflect God by Admiring His Creation....................45

10 Days of Killing Envy
    How the Enemy Wants to Stop Us from Reflecting God........67

10 Days of Being a Space Saver
    Your Strength and How to Use It 89

10 Days of Letting Go of Self-Absorption
    A Common Pain Point 111

10 Days of Saying No to Manipulation
    Going to Two in Stress..135

10 Days of Growing in Discipline
    Going to One in Growth..159

Book Recommendations for Fours 185

About the Author...187

Foreword

I spent the first twenty-five years of my life secretly thinking something was wrong with me. I knew I wasn't exactly like other people; I was a little quirkier and a lot moodier. It wasn't that I wanted to be like other people—I didn't—I just didn't want my worst fear to be confirmed. I didn't want others to figure out how messed up I really was. I wanted to be seen as special, but I feared being fully seen. I lived in the shadow of shame, making a life for myself as the mistress of both scarcity and striving.

As I edged toward a quarter century, I found myself in a therapy office. "I think I have a stress problem," I told the woman I had just met. "I just need to learn how to better manage my stress." I sized up her reaction while carefully keeping my posture erect on the far edge of the couch. But underneath my poise, I was sweating, terrified that she might tell me something worse was wrong.

Instead, she began gently naming my shame. My whole life, I had been told I was "too sensitive," and so I attempted to push away that part of myself anytime it emerged. I tried to parcel away the parts of me that might show the world I really was what I most feared—irreparably flawed—and worked hard to assert the prettier parts that would prove I was worth seeing. I tried to cover up my sensitivity with striving, but the storm of shame kept me swirling in stress, too busy grasping for security to see that who I was and where I was were already good.

I thought I was bad at dealing with stress; it turns out I had been shaming myself within it. I had spent most of life unknowingly seeing myself through lenses of shame, but my therapist helped me notice my glasses, carefully wipe them off, and begin to see the world and myself with clarity and kindness. In those sessions, she made room for my shame to be soothed and my sensitivity to be seen. My husband and I had been pretty convinced that my problem was my relationship with stress, but my therapist showed me it was my relationship with myself that needed healing.

Learning about my sensitivity led me to consider my personality with curiosity and compassion rather than judgment. And after a year and half of mistyping myself as an Enneagram One, my husband and I were finally able to see the empath at the center of my story. The more I explored my story as a type Four, the freer I became to show up in my life with a sense of security and a willingness to slowly savor the goodness that is already here.

The hidden story of my own journey from shame to security, though, was my therapist's willingness to make that journey first and to invite me onto the path too. She knew there was enough space for my specialness, sorrow, shame, and story to exist alongside hers.

Abundance tells us a truer story than shame. For Enneagram Fours, shame is a siren song. It pulls us from the present and keeps us stuck in stress, a state of scarcity, and an unending stream of striving. But God sings a stronger song. In every bud, bloom, and body, God rejoices over us with singing, pulling this present world into the redemption of His love. The ever-present possibility of hearing God's song, His delight to be with you, around you, and to redeem this world slowly, carefully, and personally is your inheritance in Jesus. Shame screams a siren song that there's no room for us to be seen, but God sings over us with love. Will we listen?

What my therapist offered me in those sessions is what Elisabeth offers you here. From her own journey from shame to abundance, Elisabeth guides us with gentle reflections to listen to the stronger song of God's love. She asks us to pay attention to the present moment as a place God is actually present. The simple reflections within this book are an invitation to set aside scarcity, shame, and striving, and instead listen to the stronger song of God's real, present love in both your soul and His world. And as you hear the melody of God's love, you'll find yourself joining the chorus, willing to let your voice be heard, in all its subtlety and strength—to let your sensitive soul be seen.

Let Elisabeth's words enfold you in this stronger song, and then keep singing. Let her words guide you even farther, into an exploration of your own story and God's song of love toward this world. Once you finish this short collection, go deeper. Find Enneagram books that will help you keep walking down the path of abundance and presence, like *The Enneagram: The Discernment of Spirits* by Richard Rohr. Let the song of God's love become the habit of your heart.

There is a stronger song than shame.
There is a place on this path for you.
There is space for your soul to be seen.
There is room for your voice in this song.

—K.J. Ramsey, licensed professional counselor
Author, *This Too Shall Last:
Finding Grace When Suffering Lingers*

Acknowledgments

My journey from young hopeful writer, all the way back to the tender age of four, to holding books with my name on them hasn't been easy or pretty. In fact, it's held a lot of hurt, disappointment, and rejection. However, as you hold a book with my name on the cover in your hands, I'd love you to know who and what has sustained me through it all. You are holding a piece of God's redemption in my story, tangible proof of His kindness, and testament of His faithfulness. I didn't break any doors down, or *do* anything myself that ensured my trajectory of publishing. God in His kindness handed me this opportunity, and to Him alone belongs all the glory and praise.

My agent, Amanda, deserves the highest of thanks and admiration. Thank you for answering my many questions, guiding, and giving me the confidence to do this. I couldn't have done it without you. To all the people at Whitaker House, my editor, Peg, and publisher, Christine, thank you for making these devotionals what they are today. It's been a pleasure working with you all.

To my writing community hope*writers, thank you for giving me the courage to call myself a writer long before I felt like one. To Christine Rollings, who has never failed to show up with encouragement and support even though we have never met in person, I feel like I know you, and I am so glad to call you friend. To Alison Bradley whose words have been such an encouragement to me as a Four. I'm so thankful to share your supportive, convicting words and wisdom with other Fours who I'm sure will find them like water in a dry place, as I have. Thank you for writing in this devotional, and giving it your heart and soul. To K.J. Ramsey, thank you for writing such a lovely foreword! It means so much that you were one of the first pair of eyes to see this devotional, and I'm so thankful for your gentle invitation to greater self-awareness. Thank you to Pastor Bubba Jennings at Resurrection Church for reading over my proposal and giving me advice on how to serve Jesus well in this process.

The people who have been the biggest support and help to me during this process, and if I'm honest, my life, are:

My Four-ish Instagram community at @4ish_andiknowit, thank you for giving me a space to learn, share, and just be a Four with you all! We truly are a special breed in the best of ways.

To all the Fours who have encouraged, space saved, and helped me feel less alone: Mikayla Larson, Abby Thompson, Emily P. Freeman, K. J. Ramsey, Audrey Bailey, Andrew Peterson, my type Four coaching clients, and many other suspected Fours that I won't publicly *type* here. Thank you!

Sarah Upton, thank you for faithfully helping with Wellington during this entire journey. I am so comfortable when he is with you, and I adore how much you love him.

Mikayla Larson, thank you for your friendship, support, and for being here when I've needed you the most. You are such a gift in my life.

John and Jan Bennett, thank you for faithfully praying for me and supporting me through this entire process. Your encouragement has moved mountains and sustained me on the hardest days.

Thank you, Mom and Dad (Joe and Diane Upton), for literally teaching me to read and write, and encouraging me to say yes to big things. I would never have had the foundation to say yes without you, and how you raised me. I'm so proud and grateful to have the two of you in my corner cheering me on.

Peter, you've been beyond supporting, patient, and caring towards me. You have taught me so much about what it means to be faithful, and you never let me quit. You believe in me enough for both of us, and I can't believe the gift that you are in my life. You're my best friend and I love you.

Introduction
What Is the Enneagram?

The Enneagram is an ancient personality typology for which no one really knows the origins.

It uses nine points within a circle—the word itself means "a drawing of nine"—to represent nine distinct personality types. The points are numbered simply to differentiate between them, with each point having no greater or less value than the others. The theory is that a person assumes one of these personalities in childhood as a reaction to discovering the world as a scary, unkind place and thus, unlikely to accept his or her true self.

The nine types are identified by their numbers or by these names:

1. The Perfectionist
2. The Helper
3. The Achiever
4. The Individualist
5. The Thinker
6. The Guardian
7. The Enthusiast
8. The Challenger
9. The Peacemaker

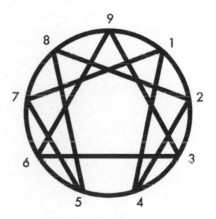

HOW DO I FIND MY TYPE?

Your Enneagram type is determined by your main motivation. Finding your Enneagram type is a journey, as we are typically unaware of our motivations and instead focus on our behaviors. Many online tests focus around behaviors, and while some motivations *may* produce certain behaviors, that may not always be the case and you are unlikely to get accurate results.

To find your Enneagram type, you need to start by learning about *all* nine Enneagram types, and explore their motivations in contrast to your own behaviors and deeper motivations.

You can ask for feedback from those around you, but most often, the more you learn, the clearer your core number shines through.

It's often the number whose description makes you feel the most *exposed* that is your true core type. You core Enneagram number won't change, since it's solidified in childhood.

Each number's distinct motivation:

1. Integrity – Goodness
2. Love – Relationships
3. Worth – Self-Importance
4. Authenticity – Unique Identity
5. Competency – Objective Truth
6. Security – Guidance
7. Satisfaction – Freedom
8. Independence – Control
9. Peace – Equilibrium

IS THIS JOURNEY WORTH IT?

Yes! The self-awareness you gain along the way is gold, and learning about the other types in the process brings you so much empathy and understanding for all of the other personalities in your life.

WHAT MAKES THE ENNEAGRAM UNIQUE AND DIFFERENT FROM MYERS-BRIGGS, STRENGTHSFINDER, OR DISC ASSESSMENTS?

The Enneagram, unlike the other typology systems mentioned, is fluid. Yes, the Enneagram tells you what your base personality characteristics are, but it also reveals how you change when you're growing, stressed, secure, unhealthy, healthy, etc.

You are not the same person at twenty as you are at sixty. You're not the same person at your stressful workplace as you are when binge-watching your favorite TV show and eating ice cream at home. The Enneagram accounts for these inconsistencies and changes in your behavior and informs you of when/how those changes occur.

If you look at the graph below, you'll see that each of the numbers connects to two other numbers by arrows. The arrow pointed toward your number is your growth arrow; the arrow pointed away is your stress number. When your life leaves you with more room to breathe, you exhibit positive characteristics of your growth number, and when you're stretched thin in seasons of stress, you exhibit the negative characteristics of your stress number.

This is one explanation for big shifts in personality over a lifetime.

Another point of difference between the Enneagram and other typology systems is *wings*. Your wings are the two numbers on either side of your core number, which add flavor to your per-

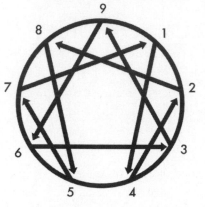

sonality type. Although your core number won't change—and your main motivation, sin proclivities, and personality will come from that core number—your wings can be very influential on your overall personality and how it presents itself. There are many different theories about wings, but the viewpoint we hold to is:

1. Your wing can only be one of the two numbers on either side of your number. Therefore, you can be a 4 with a 5 wing (4w5) but not a 4 with an 8 wing (4w8).

2. You have access to the numbers on either side of your number, but most people will only have one dominant wing. (*Dominant* meaning you exhibit more of the behaviors of one wing than the other wing.) It is possible to have equal wings or no wing at all, but this is rare.

3. Your dominant wing number can change from one to the other throughout your life, but it's speculated this might only happen once.

As you read through this book, we will go over what an Enneagram Four looks like with both of its wings. If you're struggling to figure out what your core number is, this book series could really help give you some more in-depth options!

HOW DO YOU BECOME YOUR TYPE?

Personality is a kind of shield we pick up and hide behind. It is functional, even protective at times, but altogether unnecessary because God made us in His image from the start. However, we cling to this personality like it's our key to survival, and nothing has proven us wrong so far. It's the only tool we've ever had, and the shield has scratches and dents to prove its worth.

Not all parts of our personality are wrong or bad, but by living in a fallen, sinful world, we all tend to distort even good things in bad ways. Amen?

What personality did you pick up in childhood? If you're reading this devotional, then you may have chosen type Four. You chose your shield because your need to be loved became the one thing that your life revolved around from early childhood until right now, at this very moment.

The Enneagram talks about childhood wounds and how we pick up a particular shield as a reaction to these wounds. However, not all siblings have the same Enneagram type even though they heard the same wounding message or had the same harmful experiences growing up. This is because we are born with our own unique outlook on the world, and we filter everything through that outlook. You and your siblings may have heard the same things, but while you heard, "You're only loved when there's no conflict in your life," your sibling heard, "You're only loved when you're successful." Thus, you both would become different Enneagram types.

Trauma and abuse of any kind can definitely impact your choice of shield as well. If you think of all these nine shields as being a different color, perhaps you were born predisposed to be more likely to pick blue than red. However, in a moment of early trauma, you might have heard someone shouting, "Pick black! Black is the only option!" Thus, you chose black instead of blue, which would've been your own unique reaction to your life circumstances. It's hard to say how these things happen exactly, especially when trauma is involved. Are you who you are *despite* trauma or because of it? Only God knows, but there is healing and growth to be found either way.

We've all heard the phrase, "You can't teach an old dog new tricks." I'd like to propose that when referencing personality, it might be said, "The longer you use your personality, the harder it is to see its ineffectiveness." It's not impossible for an older person to drastically change for the better, but it will be harder for them to put down what has worked for them for so long. That's why, as we age, it can become harder and harder to even see where our personality ends and our true self begins. Even if the unhealthy parts of our personality have been ineffective, they still seem to be the only things that have worked for us.

WHY DO WE NEED THE ENNEAGRAM WHEN WE HAVE THE HOLY SPIRIT AND THE BIBLE TO GUIDE US?

The Enneagram is a helpful tool, but only when it is used as such. The Enneagram cannot save you—only Jesus can do that.

However, God made us all unique, and we all reflect Him in individual ways. Learning about these unique reflections can encourage us, as well as point us toward our purposes. The Enneagram also reveals the sin problems and blind spots you may unknowingly struggle with. Revealing these blind spots leads us to repentance and change before God.

HOW DO I CHANGE MY MORE NEGATIVE BEHAVIORS?

Alcoholics Anonymous was really on to something when they called their first step "admitting you have a problem." How do you solve a problem if you don't know you have one or are in denial about it? You can't. If you have a shield you're using to protect yourself from the world, but are blissfully unaware of its existence, you won't understand how its very existence impacts you and your relationships. You definitely won't be putting that battered but battle-tested shield of a personality down anytime soon.

Similar to the wisdom of admitting one has a problem before recovery can begin, the Enneagram proposes self-knowledge as the starting point before there can be change.

You may realize you're very different from everyone else, but you may not know just how unique and *Individualist* you are. Whether you're 100 percent sure you're a Four, or just curious about the possibility, this is what it looks like to be a Four.

What It Means to Be an Individualist

I spent a lot of my teen years in the woods behind my house. I would put my headphones in, my boots on, and just get lost in the crunch of the leaves under my feet and the giant evergreens towering above me. Here, I could pretend I was in an elven forest, a music video, or just be myself, dancing like no one was watching. I often refer to those woodland hours as *running* or *going for a walk*, but in reality, there was much more to it. Those woods were my escape, and I spent a lot of my time there. Not that my home life was bad, it was actually quite wonderful, but I still didn't feel understood—not by my parents, by my friends, or even by myself.

But when nobody was watching, the girl in the woods didn't have to be herself. She could pretend to be someone people seemed to understand.

Listening to certain songs now can send me back to those days, remembering the smell of the trees after a rainstorm, the calm of moments between songs, and the uncertainty of being fourteen and not knowing what life held in the years ahead.

Once I moved out of my parents' house, my heart often yearned to return to that old escape, but as I adapted to life without it, I slowly learned I was 100 percent loved and understood just as I was. Not by my husband, my parents, or even myself, but by my Creator, who created that young girl as somebody who never needed to escape from Him.

I am an Enneagram Four, the Individualist.

Fours are considered to be one of the rarest numbers on the Enneagram, and that's just the way they like it. Fours are called Individualists because they are motivated by being authentic, with a focus on the past and an idealistic view of the present and future. However, this idealist mentality means that Fours can become frustrated by reality, often needing to escape into their romantic or creative thoughts about how the present, the future, or even they themselves could be different.

Fours grow up believing something is wrong with them, that they are missing something. Why is everyone else so likable ... and I'm not? Why is everyone so talented ... and I'm not? Why is it so easy for everyone else to become themselves?

Fours are very socially aware but also tend not to conform to social norms, making them appear somewhat awkward or different. Because Fours are aware of *being* different, they assume they'll be rejected in social groups before they actually are rejected. This mentality becomes a self-fulfilling prophecy, and Fours use it to confirm their own negative thoughts and feelings about their likability.

To Fours, being trendy or socially normal can feel inauthentic—if everyone else is doing it, then they are being influenced, and it's not their genuine choice. This inner dialogue gives Fours a bit of a thrill whenever they discover something about themselves that is rare or unique, even if it's something simple like eye color, blood type, or birth date.

Fours have a love of beauty that translates into being quite creative; imaginative expression will look different for each Four, but it is fair to assume that there are quite a few Fours who are famous musicians, artists, photographers, writers, and creative people of all kinds. Creativity is one of the ways that, like a little child with a beloved parent, Fours look to creator God and say, "I want to be like You."

If I had known about the Enneagram in my formative years, those feelings about myself would have been much less condemning. I would realize, *Oh, sweet girl, being a young Four is hard, but you don't need to hide.* I didn't have the language of the Enneagram back then. It wasn't until I was twenty-one that I discovered this helpful tool. Since then, it has turned a lot of my *What's wrong with me?* thoughts into a deeper understanding of myself, the people around me, and the God who created all of us to reflect Him. I hope this devotional helps you do the same.

All About Being a Four

MOTIVATION

Authenticity

A Four's main motivation in life is to find their most authentic self and live out life as that person.

BIGGEST FEAR

Having no unique significance

Fours fear that all of their desires and dreams have already been accomplished or could be done better by someone else. This leaves a Four feeling purposeless and proves their fears of worthlessness.

HEART TRIAD

Each Enneagram type is dominant in either feeling, thinking, or doing. These *triads* are referred to as heart-centered, head-centered, and gut-centered.

Fours, along with Twos and Threes, are part of the heart triad. This means that they first process information as feelings before moving on to thinking or doing. In the most practical sense, others' actions tend to feel very personal, as a Four first processes information as feeling before it can be thought about logically. Those in the heart triad may be told they are too sensitive.

Each of the three triads also has a defining emotion connected to the center they use most.

For the heart triad, this emotion is *shame*. Twos, Threes, and Fours struggle to believe that they have inherent worth, so they believe that they must *do* something in order to have worth.

As we know from Scripture, God knew us before He formed us in our mother's womb (see Jeremiah 1:5) and He gave us worth. Our worth cannot be taken away from us, we cannot earn it, and we cannot add more worth to ourselves by doing anything.

> *Look at the birds of the air: they neither sow nor reap nor gather into barns, and yet your heavenly Father feeds them. Are you not of more value than they?* (Matthew 6:26)

Of course, we are worth more than birds. God made us in His own image, with thoughts, feelings, desires, and dominion here on earth.

> *So God created man in his own image, in the image of God he created him; male and female he created them. And God blessed them. And God said to them, "Be fruitful and multiply and fill the earth and subdue it, and have dominion over the fish of the sea and over the birds of the heavens and over every living thing that moves on the earth."*
> (Genesis 1:27–28)

God formed you, put the breath in your lungs, and gave you value here on earth. Those of us in the heart triad often doubt that value, but it's undeniable.

Shame comes into play when Satan uses the lie, "You'll never be worth anything" to paralyze Fours and condemn them. If he cannot destroy you and your future, Satan will try to steal your peace and the good works God has set before you to do.

CHILDHOOD WOUND

The wounding message Fours heard (or thought they heard) as children was, "It is not okay to be too much or not enough."

This message contributes to many of Fours' internal paradoxes, such as push-pull relationship tendencies, imposter syndrome, shame, longing for community yet looking for rejection, and a host of other internal heartaches.

THE LOST CHILDHOOD MESSAGE FOURS LONG TO HEAR

"You are seen (and loved) for who you are"

When Fours rest in the fact that Jesus both fully sees them and loves them, they can silence their shame, live as accepted instead of rejected, and pursue community in confidence.

DEFENSE MECHANISM

Introjection (internalizing criticism or negative information)

This is the behavior we use when we are on the defensive or stressed. Introjection (internalizing criticism or negative information) is a counter-intuitive defense mechanism in which a person incorporates negative data from others into their sense of self.

Here is an example of introjection: if someone tells you that you are a horrible driver, instead of trying harder to become a better driver, you might introject and resign yourself to being a bad driver. It's a way to self-inflict criticism instead of having to deal with criticism from an outside source; you might even bring up this "fact" before someone else points it out. The odd thing about introjection is that Fours do not do it for positive reinforcement. Instead, they repel positive information or compliments by insisting, "That person just doesn't know me," or "That may be true of me now, but not always."

WINGS

As I mentioned earlier, your wings are the numbers on either side of your core number that add flavor to your core Enneagram type. For Fours, this wing is either a Five or a Three. Fours can identify with both wings or no wing at all, but it's most common to have one dominant wing.

Four with a Five Wing (4w5)

A Four's creativity and a Five's investigative nature make for quite the daydreamer when combined as a 4w5. More reserved than other Fours, a 4w5 can surprise others with emotional depth, knowledge about favorite topics, and the way they are able to articulate feelings when they feel comfortable enough to open up. In fact, many 4w5s will be mistyped as Fives, Sixes, or Nines by those who don't know them well. A 4w5, like their Enneagram sibling 5w4, will wrestle with the tension between logical and emotional feelings.

Four with a Three Wing (4w3)

Fours with a Three wing are creatively ambitious and social, with have lots of competitive energy. In *The Road Back to You*, authors Ian Morgan Cron and Suzanne Stabile note, "Fours with a dominant Three wing want to be both the most unique *and* the best."[1] This is quite the motivation for success!

These Fours struggle with the people-pleasing nature of their Three wing, and their souls cry out for true authenticity. When a 4w3 creates, they want their creation to be seen and admired by others more than the average Four or a 4w5 would. Being very image-conscious, a 4w3 will hide some of the quirkiness of their core number; they can often be mistyped as a Three, Seven, or Eight.

ARROWS

Your arrows are the two numbers your Enneagram number are connected to in the Enneagram diagram. These two arrows represent the number from which you get the best traits as you grow, or the number from which you get the worst traits when you're in seasons of stress.

Stress: Going to Two

In stress, a Four's fixation on what is missing in their life becomes relational as they pick up the unhealthy behaviors of a Two. A stressed Four will dwell on favors, gifts, or kind gestures that are unrepaid, and may even try to bait people they admire into affirming them.

1. Ian Morgan Cron and Suzanne Stabile, *The Road Back to You* (Downers Grove, IL: InterVarsity Press, 2016).

Growth: Going to One

In growth, normally emotional Fours gain the logical, organized, and dutiful behaviors of a healthy One. A Four who is growing isn't as easily overtaken by their feelings, withdrawn, or given to emotional outbursts as an unhealthy Four. Instead, the One energy they have access to in growth helps them to logically work through their emotions or envy and gives them the motivation to improve the world with their creative gifts.

TYPE FOUR SUBTYPES

When we talk about subtypes and the Enneagram, we are referring to three relational instincts we all have. These instincts, like those of *fight or flight*, are reactions over which we have little control. The three relational subtypes are Self-Preservation (Sp), Social (So), and One-to-One (Sx). We all have the capacity to use all three of these instincts, but one of them is usually dominant, and that dominant subtype can strongly impact how your distinct Enneagram type looks to everyone else.

Bubbly Four (Sp)

Self-Preservation Fours still have all the deep emotions of other Fours, but they don't communicate emotions (envy, suffering, etc.) as other Fours do. Instead of vocally using their suffering to gain attention, Sp subtypes take a more long-suffering approach to life. They hope this long-suffering will be admired by others, but that's not their main goal. At a very young age, these Fours might have learned that displaying intense emotions makes others uncomfortable, so they put on a stoic or bubbly front instead.

The Romantic Four (So)

Social Fours look the most like regular Fours, and, as a result, they rarely mistype. Social Fours find comfort in melancholy and suffering. Beatrice Chestnut explains, "They hope that if their suffering is sufficiently recognized and understood, they might be forgiven for their failures and deficiencies and loved unconditionally."[2] Of course, this is a distortion of the truth that Fours are *already* fully known and loved by God, and that His love isn't dependent on their perception of their wholeness. These Fours are less competitive and focus more on their place within social groups. They fear being disconnected and out of the community, but once they're in social situations, they compare themselves to others and assume they are rejected before they actually are.

The Passionate Four (Sx)

One-to-One Fours look more like Eights because they're competitive, they brave conflict without fear, and, instead of punishing themselves for their shame, they tend to subconsciously punish others. This punishment can be administered by withholding emotion, affection, invitations, or assistance to those they deem undeserving. What separates this type from Eights is their deep connection to their feelings, internal shame, and how desperately they desire approval from those relationships closest to them.

---

2. "Social Four description (according to Beatrice Chestnut)," Personality Café (www.personalitycafe.com/type-4-forum-individualist/214202-social-four-description-according-beatrice-chestnut.html).

So I'm a Four. What Now?

Why should I, as a type Four, embark on sixty days of devotions?

Whether you have just realized you are a type Four on the Enneagram, or have known it for some time, you've probably thought, *Okay, but what now? I get that I'm an individualist, that I crave authenticity, and that I'm a heart-centered romantic who struggles with comparison and envy. The question is, how do I take this self-awareness and turn it into practical transformation?*

Some Enneagram teachers will tell you that you need only to focus on self-actualization and pull yourself up by your proverbial boot-straps to grow out of your worst behaviors. "Meditate!" they say. "Focus on yourself!" Yet, at the same time they tell you, "Stop being so self-absorbed!"

However, I'm here to offer a different foundation for growth. As Christians, we know that we are flawed, sinful, and far from God's intended plan for humanity. The hymn "Come Thou Fount of Every Blessing," includes the lyrics, "Prone to wander, Lord I feel it!" This speaks to the reality of our hearts and their rebellious nature toward our Savior.

This wandering is the problem, sin is the problem, and we are the problem! So, anyone who tells us that we ought to focus on ourselves to find growth will only lead us to more confusion. We may even find ourselves back where we started as we go around and around this idea of focusing on self.

But we are not without hope. Philippians 1:6 says, "*I am sure of this, that he who began a good work in you will bring it to completion at the day of Jesus Christ.*" On the very day you acknowledged Jesus as your Savior, repented from your sin, and dedicated your life to Him, He began a good work in your life. This work is called *sanctification*, which is the act of becoming holy. Your sanctification will not be finished here on earth, but you are in the process of *becoming*, day by day, moment by moment, only by the Holy Spirit's work and power within you.

We might not know how to articulate it, but this work of sanctification is the growth and change for which we long. All of us know we are not who we want to be. Reflecting on the human condition in Romans 7:15, Paul said, "*For I do not understand my own actions. For I do not do what I want, but I do the very thing I hate.*" Isn't that the truth? I don't want to envy others, but the yucky feeling in the pit of my stomach is something I know well.

We all know we have this haunting *potential* that always seems just a little out of reach. We all have this nagging feeling that we were created for more ... but how do we get there? Only by God's grace and power within us can we rest in His sanctifying work and trust Him for the growth and potential of bringing glory to Him. Only God can sanctify us, but it is our responsibility to be "*slaves of righteousness*" (Romans 6:18) and obey Him.

Over the next sixty days, we want to take you day by day through what God says about your specific problems as a Four, and how He wants to lovingly sanctify you into being more like Jesus.

The lens of the Enneagram gives us a great starting point for your specific pain points and strengths. We will use those to encourage you in the areas where God is reflected through you and in the areas where you need to lay down your instincts and let Him change you.

Some of these topics might be hard, but we hope you'll let the tension you feel in your heart open you up to change. This is where obedience comes in. We all have blind spots and areas we are more comfortable leaving in the dark, but God desires so much more for us. So ask Him to help you release your grip on those areas, bring them into the light, and experience the freedom repentance offers.

Understand me, I'm begging you.
Just a glimmer of recognition, just a word of encouragement.
I jump back, pained when you finally reach out a hand.
Leave me alone, let me do this on my own.

There is this nagging ache, a hole in my soul.
Maybe I wasn't finished before I was born.
A missing piece; yeah, that sounds like me.
Never quite finished, never measuring up.
What's wrong with me?

How does everyone else do this? How are they all so happy?
It's maddening how different I feel, so lonely to be the only me.

I walk the way I walk; I think the way I think; yes, there's a peace in being unique.

Every emotion deserves a home, and I guess I'm taking in strays.
Sadness, despair, guilt, yes, envy too.
Get in the truck; I've been expecting you.
If I spend too much time with happiness, they all get angry; gotta love them all equally.
Melancholy is cold but beautiful. Demanding respect.
Deep down, I know I like her best.

This is how chaotic and beautiful it is to be me.
The individualist, a true Four, this is me.

—*Elisabeth Bennett*

Your Guides For This Journey

You'll be hearing from two other writers and Enneagram coaches in the days ahead. The days in which no author is listed are written by me. On other days, I have asked these two Enneagram experts to help you on your path.

CHRISTINE ROLLINGS

Christine is an Enneagram Two with a desire to help people understand themselves and have the words to express their story to others. This led her to become an Enneagram coach, after finding the Enneagram helpful for naming her own strengths, longings, and struggles. She works particularly with people living cross-culturally, with their particular set of challenges and joys. Having her growth arrow pointing toward type Four not only gives her a depth of understanding of Fours' strengths, but also a great appreciation of them.

ALISON BRADLEY

Alison is the Enneagram Nine who has taught me so much about appreciating my strengths as a Four. She has a deep love for the Lord and a wealth of understanding and compassion towards the more emotional parts of life. She has recently become an Enneagram coach and has a great deal of knowledge about this entire typology.

10 Days of Finding Beauty in Life
How We Reflect God by Admiring His Creation

● ● ● ● ● ● ● ● ● ● ● ● **DAY 1**

How You Reflect God

> *The heavens declare the glory of God,*
> *and the sky above proclaims his handiwork.*
> (Psalm 19:1)

Dearest Individualist, did you know you uniquely reflect God? Like a child leaning down to see the reflection of their face in a pond, we reflect the image of our heavenly Father. Now, this doesn't mean we have a body like His, but that we reflect parts of God's character to the rest of the world. It's not a perfect reflection—in fact, it's rippled and marred. However, a familiarity, a family resemblance, is still plainly evident between God and His creation.

We were made in the image of God, as Genesis 1:27 tells us: *"So God created man in his own image, in the image of God he created him; male and female he created them."*

God made us in His image. He didn't have to, but He gave us each unique parts of Himself. Unlike human parents who don't get to choose which part of their genetic make-up is passed on to their children, God chose exactly which parts of Himself we would receive. There is something so special and awe-inspiring about that.

When *you* create, you're reflecting our creative God. When you give, you're reflecting our generous God. Even when you're

45

admiring a sunset above the ocean, you're reflecting our God's love of beauty.

I find that it's easy to focus on the ways in which we *don't* reflect God. Our sin is often so loud and shameful in demanding center stage with the thoughts we have about ourselves.

However, have you ever considered that dwelling on the ways in which we do reflect God brings glory to Him?

Like a proud father who brags about his child's athletic ability that mirrors his own, God is delighted in the ways in which we reflect Him. Thinking about this reflection, and thanking Him for it, helps us to develop the right attitude toward our humanity. We are humble, small, fickle, and sinful. Yet, we are also created, adopted, and loved beyond measure.

SHIFT IN FOCUS

Spend a couple of moments reflecting on and thanking God for the ways in which you reflect Him.

Dear heavenly Father, thank You for making me like You. Help me to notice more and more, every day, the gifts You have given me, and how I can glorify You with them. I want others to look at me and see a glimmer of You. Thank You for helping me do that. Amen.

What is your favorite reflection of God that you can see in yourself? Jot it down and post it somewhere to remind yourself how you are uniquely like Him.

● ● ● ● ● ● ● ● ● ● ● ● **DAY 2**

Our God's Original, Beautiful Design

And God said, "Behold, I have given you every plant yielding seed
that is on the face of all the earth, and every tree with seed in its
fruit. You shall have them for food. And to every beast of the earth
and to every bird of the heavens and to everything that creeps on the
earth, everything that has the breath of life, I have given every green
plant for food." And it was so. And God saw everything that he had
made, and behold, it was very good.
(Genesis 1:29–31)

Have you ever thought about how creative God is? Every beautiful sunset, every waterfall, every majestic animal, and every miraculous human body was created by God; their very existence proclaims His glory. Those things were all here before humanity's fall, and because our God is so gracious to us, they are still here now.

God cares about beautiful things. He didn't slap us together and say, "That'll work." No, instead He said, "This is *very good.*" Everything He made in the beginning was very good, and very good is still His desire for His creation.

As humans, we instinctively know when we see God's good design. This is why we get that feeling of awe when we see a sunset, or a feeling of satisfaction when we look at something with an intricate design. That's how God intended everything to be, and our soul is at rest and at home in His beautiful creation.

As an Enneagram Four, you probably nod your head as you view God's beauty around you. Noticing His wonderful creation comes naturally to you. You feel at home in nature and in lovely spaces. You want to emulate God by creating and adding your own enticing perspective to the world. These are all things that come second nature to you because you are reflecting God's very own creative, beauty-loving nature.

When you notice and focus on those things that reflect God's perfect design for the world—beauty in nature, happy emotions, savory foods, good health, pleasing music—you are agreeing with God on His original plan for us, and you have an opportunity to rejoice with hope in the things to come that He has prepared for you.

SHIFT IN FOCUS

Take a moment to pray:

God, I praise You for Your beautiful design, and how You uniquely wired me to enjoy and seek this beauty. Today, I pray that You will help me to notice more of what is good rather than what is wrong, and that my heart would rejoice as I agree with You about what is good. Amen.

Use your five senses to notice what is good around you:

God, thank You for designing _____, which is good, and I can enjoy its taste.

God, thank You for designing _____, which is good, and I can enjoy its smell.

God, thank You for designing _____, which is good, and I can enjoy its feel.

God, thank You for designing _____, which is good, and I can enjoy seeing it.

God, thank You for designing _____, which is good, and I can enjoy hearing it.

DAY 3 • • • • • • • • • • •

Remnants of Beauty Still Here

In his hand are the depths of the earth, and the mountain peaks
belong to him. The sea is his, for he made it,
and his hands formed the dry land.
(Psalm 95:4–5 NIV)

Do you enjoy watching nature documentaries as much as I do? Although I admit that the whole predator/prey aspect of wildlife can stress me out, there is something soothing and wonderful about seeing places and animals that I would otherwise never get to see. My Dad always enjoyed nature documentaries, especially underwater ones, so I grew up watching *Planet Earth* many times over. Even as a child, technology was bringing the world to my living room, and my admiration of its beauty is still as fresh as the first time I saw those videos.

Have you ever thought about how much of the garden of Eden might still be here? When Adam and Eve were cast out of man's natural habitat, the earth was cursed. We now have an aversion to work, and we suffer through painful childbirth. There are tragedies, diseases, and natural disasters. However, in the midst of the bad that came from the fall, you'll find remnants of the good—remnants of Eden and of God's breathtaking original creation.

As a Four, you've probably been searching for these remnants, romanticizing about seeing these great wonders without realizing how connected to God this desire is. It is by God's grace that mountains, flowers, majestic animals, crystal-clear waters, and thick forests are still here for us to marvel at and enjoy. These things can help us feel close to God because they're His gifts to us.

SHIFT IN FOCUS

Set a timer for three minutes and write down all the things in Eden that we still get to enjoy today. Spend some time thanking God for these things and asking Him to help you notice them more.

DAY 4 • • • • • • • • • •

We Reflect His Love of Beauty When We Admire What He Made Beautiful

See, I have called by name Bezalel the son of Uri, son of Hur, of the tribe of Judah, and I have filled him with the Spirit of God, with ability and intelligence, with knowledge and all craftsmanship, to devise artistic designs, to work in gold, silver, and bronze, in cutting stones for setting, and in carving wood, to work in every craft. (Exodus 31:2–5)

Over the past couple of years, I've embarked on a Bible reading plan. Every October, as the leaves begin to fall and the air smells earthy, sweet, and musky, I read through Exodus and Leviticus in the Old Testament. In those books, you can't help but notice God's love for beauty, not only human beauty, but also the beauty of architecture, nature, and fashion.

God had big design plans for His tabernacle, and they were relayed in *painstaking* detail, from the square footage and interior design to the garments the priests were to wear. God had a beautiful design for all of them. We even see in the verse above that He filled workers like Bezalel with His Spirit to enable them to work with skill beyond their training or natural talent. That's how much God cares about beauty and design. In addition, God's Spirit knows how to sew, paint, weave, and carve. Isn't that wonderful?

Dear Four, can you see this love of beauty reflected in your life? Have you spent more hours in Home Depot's paint aisle than you can count? Do you enjoy putting together unique outfits to wear, maybe even sewing them yourself? Do you use your hands to turn something beautiful into a still image others can enjoy forever? There are so many ways your love of beauty can manifest itself, and I don't want you to discount this love as something meaningless or *less than*. Your love of beauty was placed within you by the Creator Himself. He gave you this love purposefully, and it was meant to bring glory to our God—the ultimate lover of beauty.

SHIFT IN FOCUS

Is there an area of your life where you can see your love of beauty shining through?

This week, I took a paint chip and wrote down four ways that I see my love of beauty reflecting God's love of beauty.

I listed:

- Words
- Graphic Design
- Hair/Makeup
- Clothes

Then, I taped this paint chip to the front of my notebook. It can be encouraging as a nontraditional artist—one with no musical or customary artistic talent—to see the ways I'm creative displayed in front of me. I'm creative; I make things beautiful; I am an artist who reflects my artistic God.

DAY 5 • • • • • • • • • •

We Help Others See God Through His Creation

And I have given to all able men ability, that they may make all that I have commanded you.
(Exodus 31:6)

One of the coolest things about being a Four is how others appreciate our gifts. So many of the artistic industries, such as music, film, fashion, and photography, are dominated by type Fours. Our heartbeat is to create, reflecting our creative Creator. And create we do!

Of course, it's not just Fours who enjoy a sappy, dramatic, sad song every now and then. Nor are Fours the only ones who enjoy performing, painting, architecture, and literature. All people enjoy these things, and every other Enneagram number is enriched by what Fours add to the world.

Humankind is drawn to music, nature, and other arts because there is a heartbeat, something so alive, within these. We often mistake this heartbeat as belonging to the artist, but it really belongs to God. Even when art is not God-honoring, it still, in and of itself, reflects a God who shows us what true art looks like through His creation.

When we worship an artist, it often results in the artist becoming miserable under the weight of glory, which is something we were never designed to bear. However, when we humbly allow ourselves to be the conduit by which honor and glory flow straight to God, we can live in the peace of our true purpose.

As Fours, we are responsible for what we do with glory. You may not think your life is very glorious, but look closer. You may receive a small taste of glory with compliments, or your first sale on Etsy, or applause after you speak on a stage, or thousands of likes on social media. Wherever you are in your journey, dear Four, glory is knocking at your door. No matter how much more glorious others' lives seem, you have something special, and glory has been a part of your past and will remain a part of your future. Will you kill yourself under the weight of it or will you freely offer it up to your Creator?

SHIFT IN FOCUS

Can you identify an area in your life in which you feel like you're being crushed by expectations?

What would it look like to rest in the Lord, giving Him both the weight and the glory for your artistic gifts?

DAY 6 • • • • • • • • • • •

God's Creation Brings Us to Our Knees

Why is light given to him who is in misery, and life to the bitter in soul, who long for death, but it comes not, and dig for it more than for hidden treasures, who rejoice exceedingly and are glad when they find the grave?
(Job 3:20–22)

As a Four, I really relate to the book of Job. This godly man was so special that Satan had a vendetta against him. Then, when everything came crashing down, Job was comfortable in his sadness and anger. I'm not saying that Job was a Four—I don't think we can accurately type Bible characters—but his lament, which makes up Job 3–31, feels familiar to my inner world.

No matter how familiar you are with Job's story, have you ever read God's reply to Job's lament? It sends chills down my spine every time I read it. It's beautiful and reality-crushing at the same time.

Take a moment to read a portion of what God tells Job:

Have you comprehended the expanse of the earth? Declare, if you know all this. Where is the way to the dwelling of light, and where is the place of darkness, that you may take it to its territory and that you may discern the paths to its home? You know, for you were born then, and the number of your days is great! Have you entered the storehouses of the snow, or have you seen the storehouses of the hail, which

I have reserved for the time of trouble, for the day of battle and war? What is the way to the place where the light is distributed, or where the east wind is scattered upon the earth? Who has cleft a channel for the torrents of rain and a way for the thunderbolt, to bring rain on a land where no man is, on the desert in which there is no man, to satisfy the waste and desolate land, and to make the ground sprout with grass? (Job 38:18–27)

God's questions awake Job to a reality that is much bigger than what he can see. The words make me feel so small, but in the best of ways. God didn't create and then forget. He did not create and then leave. He holds His creation in a thoughtful and mighty hand. He is sovereignly aware of it all.

This is why, when we admire His creation today, we are not just admiring the day He created such a magnificent universe, but also the fact that He is still sustaining it all, right now.

SHIFT IN FOCUS

Dear heavenly Father, I thank You that Your creation brings us to our knees before You. I praise You for Your sovereign hand over all of the unseen, for Your great and mighty mind that crafted all for us to enjoy. Today, please help me notice, listen, understand, and stand in awe of what You created. Instill in me a heart that longs to worship the Creator and bask in the beauty of this wonder. Amen.

If this reminder is helpful to you, you can listen to it in music form by searching for the song "Where Were You?" by Ghost Ship. It's a powerful song that gives me goose bumps every time I hear it.

DAY 7

Focusing on the Beauty Around You

Give thanks in all circumstances;
for this is the will of God in Christ Jesus for you.
(1 Thessalonians 5:18)

Do you ever catch yourself waiting to enjoy the world around you? Are you waiting for summer? Waiting for fall? Waiting for a vacation? Waiting for whichever holiday comes next?

I personally catch myself eagerly awaiting fall. Fall is the only season that I truly let myself enjoy without longing for what's next. I savor fall, while the rest of the year, I'm kind of angsty.

So you'll understand that I'm really asking myself this when I pose the question to you: what are you missing in all your waiting? What is there, right now, that's beautiful and worthy of enjoying fully without looking ahead to what comes next?

In this season—whether it be a life season or a season on the calendar—what are you missing out on by waiting, longing, and saving up your longing for another time. I don't believe God makes us wait in order to find things to be thankful for, or ways to see His creative hand at work around us. In fact, 1 Thessalonians 5:18 says, *"Give thanks in all circumstances; for this is the will of God in Christ Jesus for you."*

As a Four, one of the ways your soul gives thanks is by admiring beauty. It's how you're wired. The enemy knows this and wants to steal this joy by adding a *but* where there should've been a thankful period. I catch myself in this often:

"This campsite is amazing, *but* these mosquitoes are the worst."

"Those waves hitting the shore are breathtaking, *but* it's too hot."

However, we can redeem *but* by turning it around, by turning our waiting for the future into God-honoring thanksgiving for the now.

SHIFT IN FOCUS

Let your soul find thanksgiving by following this simple exercise:

This is what I'm waiting for:		This is what's beautiful about right now:
	BUT	
	BUT	
	BUT	

There is something right now that would bring the Lord glory if you would only notice it.

DAY 8
You Add Beauty to This World

Now there are varieties of gifts, but the same Spirit;
and there are varieties of service, but the same Lord;
and there are varieties of activities, but it is the same
God who empowers them all in everyone. To each is given the
manifestation of the Spirit for the common good.
(1 Corinthians 12:4–7)

Growing up, my creativity wasn't appreciated like an athletic gift or other forms of talent. I don't think I even verbalized how creative I was until my teen years. My creativity just wasn't valued or encouraged by those around me.

Maybe you felt this same way, or maybe your gifts have felt *less than others*. Dear Individualist, can I give you permission to think of your talents, giftings, and crafts as important? They matter, not only to your own soul, your wellbeing, and your purpose, but also to God and to the world.

Comparison wants to tell you a different story—we'll have more to say about that monster later—but hear what God is telling you: "*And there are varieties of activities, but it is the same God who empowers them all in everyone.*" God is the Author of your gifts, not you. They're not yours to be ashamed of or to degrade. God gave you the ability to create a color palette that evokes emotions, He gave you musical ability, He gave you a mind that can put feelings into beautiful words. It was He who gave you part of Himself by creating in you a unique way to make the world more beautiful.

Individualist, you add beauty to the world. I might not know you, but I do know this: no matter who told you your craft wasn't important, or how often the enemy wants to distract you with comparison, listen to the voice of your heavenly Father. He values *your thing* enough to bless the world with it through you.

SHIFT IN FOCUS

Dear heavenly Father, I thank You for the giftings You have given me. I verbally rebuke and firmly disagree with the voices that have told me my abilities were not important. I choose to rest in the fact that You gave me these abilities and that You have a plan to use them for Your glory. Help me to listen to Your voice and follow where You lead me. Amen.

DAY 9

Creativity Matters

Is not this the carpenter, the son of Mary and brother of James and Joses and Judas and Simon? And are not his sisters here with us?
(Mark 6:3)

Have you ever paused to think about Jesus and His day job? No, not as a preacher and teacher but as a carpenter. Jesus, the Son of God, was taught a trade and labored with His hands. Isn't that awesome to think about?

It's commonly thought that Jesus worked with wood. However, modern translations, teachers, and historians actually think the Greek word *tekton* that we translate as *carpenter* is more accurately translated as *craftsman*, meaning that Jesus was more likely a stonemason. Given the rock-dense landscape of ancient Israel and the lack of trees, this makes a lot of sense. So, instead of thinking of Jesus with His hands covered in sawdust, think of Him as cutting, preparing, and forming stones into useful and beautiful things.

Now, Jesus was a craftsman to provide for His family, but I'm sure He also delighted in His work. God chose exactly where Jesus would live during His life on earth, and making Him a *carpenter's son* was no afterthought. The family who raised Jesus was Hebrew, descendants of David, a humble family who worked with their hands. Jesus's life fulfilled prophecy, but it wasn't showy or grand. No doubt, Jesus left items behind that He created—practical goods that His hands formed.

The art of creating comes straight from our creative God. When you make something beautiful, you're reflecting God's creative nature. Jesus Himself did this with His work as a carpenter or stonemason, and that's not something to gloss over. Creativity is important work and reflects the very nature of God.

SHIFT IN FOCUS

What was the significance of Jesus's day job?

Do you feel understood knowing creativity and labor were a part of Jesus's life?

• • • • • • • • • • • • DAY 10

Proclaim His Glory

> *For his invisible attributes, namely, his eternal*
> *power and divine nature, have been clearly perceived, ever since*
> *the creation of the world, in the things that have been made.*
> *So they are without excuse.*
> (Romans 1:20)

When you read the verse above, what do you think about?

Another translation puts it this way:

> *By taking a long and thoughtful look at what God has cre-*
> *ated, people have always been able to see what their eyes as*
> *such can't see: eternal power, for instance, and the mystery*
> *of his divine being. So nobody has a good excuse.*
> (Romans 1:20 MSG)

It's so mysterious, awe-inspiring, and beautiful to think about how God's creation can't help but proclaim His glory. Like an artist with a unique style, God's style is something we recognize when we see it. His fingerprints are all over His creation, and you are a part of that.

Just as the Grand Canyon and the vast oceans proclaim a great Creator, so does your existence. You are marked by the fingerprints of God, you are created by Him, and you, uniquely in all His creation, reflect His characteristics to the rest of the earth. You are not just His creation—you are His child.

When you create, when you admire beauty, when you design, sing, or paint, you are proclaiming the glory of your heavenly Father to those around you. That's a humbling and grand calling, isn't it? I think it's almost paralyzing, unless we are relying on the Lord for every step of this heavy calling.

SHIFT IN FOCUS

As you think about proclaiming God's glory, and what a heavy calling that is, spend some time in prayer. Borrow these words if they reflect your heart:

> Dear heavenly Father, I thank You that I am not only Your creation but also Your child. I thank You that my very existence proclaims that You are a glorious Creator. Please remind me of this calling and humble me in it. Strengthen me to walk in Your ways and to proclaim Your glory above all else. This is my purpose, God, and I'm so thankful for it. Amen.

Meditate on these verses:

> *So as to walk in a manner worthy of the Lord, fully pleasing to him: bearing fruit in every good work and increasing in the knowledge of God; being strengthened with all power, according to his glorious might, for all endurance and patience with joy; giving thanks to the Father, who has qualified you to share in the inheritance of the saints in light.*
> (Colossians 1:10–12)

10 Days of Killing Envy

How the Enemy Wants to Stop Us from Reflecting God

● ● ● ● ● ● ● ● ● ● ● **DAY 11**

What Is a Deadly Sin?

> *If anyone is caught in any transgression, you who are spiritual*
> *should restore him in a spirit of gentleness.*
> *Keep watch on yourself, lest you too be tempted.*
> (Galatians 6:1)

Although the Bible does not mention the *seven deadly sins*, a list of them has been used by Christians for ages. The classification of these sins that we know today was first penned by Evagrius Ponticus, a monk who lived from 345 to 399 AD. This list has gone through many changes over the years, but it has remained a helpful way for us to name the vices that keep us in chains.

Each of these seven sins can be paired with an Enneagram number (with two extra sins to total nine), to give us a better idea of the specific vices that may be tripping up each type. These problem sins are often blind spots to us. Their exposure leads us to repentance and greater unity with Christ, which is the greatest thing learning about our Enneagram number can do for us.

Here are the deadly sins early Enneagram teachers paired with each type:

1. Anger
2. Pride

3. Deceit

4. Envy

5. Greed

6. Fear

7. Gluttony

8. Lust

9. Sloth

This idea of struggling with one dominant sin does not mean that you do not struggle with any or all of these sins. We can all recognize ourselves in each of those sins. However, the dominant deadly sin paired with your Enneagram type is a specific tool Satan will use to distract you from seeing how you reflect God.

For Fours, the deadly sin is envy, and whether or not you recognize envy in your own life, I encourage you to give it great thought and prayer as you read these coming chapters.

Exposing blind spots in our lives can feel a lot like ripping off a bandage that we might prefer to leave on, but what's underneath is God-honoring and beautiful.

SHIFT IN FOCUS

Spend some time contemplating and praying about what envy might look like in your life.

Does it surprise you to see that sin printed next to your Enneagram number?

• • • • • • • • • • • • DAY 12

What Is Envy?

Then I saw that all toil and all skill in work come from a man's envy
of his neighbor. This also is vanity and a striving after wind.
(Ecclesiastes 4:4)

When you think of the word *envy*, what comes to mind? One of the first things I think of is the story of Cain and Abel—a tale as old as time—a brother killing a brother because he envied him. (See Genesis 4.)

Another more personal example happened when I was six years old. I vividly remember feeling envy as I watched an older girl, who I thought was my best friend, sit in a circle with other older girls, giggling and having fun, and leaving me sitting alone at the park.

I never would have admitted I had an envy problem before I learned about the Enneagram. In reality, I just called my envy problem by other names: self-pity, pride, and anger, among many others. Somehow, calling envy something else made me feel less responsible for my feelings. Naming it envy calls out my sin.

Envy is the feeling you experience when you want something you think you deserve, but someone else—someone you deem as undeserving—already has it.

For Fours, envy has little to do with the actual item or talent others have; it has everything to do with what you think it gets them. *Likability* is something Fours often feel is just out of their reach. Satan wants us to blame others for taking all the likability in the room.

Fours are usually aware of their envy. However, to them, envy feels more like something another person is doing *to them* rather than a sinful reaction they are responsible for controlling.

To Fours, envy feels like shame and failure; it feels like someone stealing something from them. It's a very unpleasant feeling.

SHIFT IN FOCUS

Do you have a vivid memory of experiencing envy?

Did that initial feeling lead to sin in your actions, or did you go to God?

● ● ● ● ● ● ● ● ● ● ● **DAY 13**

How Satan Wants to Stop You from Reflecting God

*Be sober-minded; be watchful. Your adversary the devil prowls
around like a roaring lion, seeking someone to devour.*
(1 Peter 5:8)

Earlier in this devotional, we talked about how you reflect God
and what that means for you as a Four. But with that honor
comes a cost. We have an enemy because our God has an enemy.
This enemy, Satan, does not want God's image to reflect clearly
through us, and so he seeks to destroy us. If Satan can't have our
eternity, he will endeavor to steal our testimony, our peace, and
our joy.

To do this, Satan uses envy as Four's main temptation
because he knows it works. He knows how much Fours reflect
the love of beauty, empathy, and the creative nature of God
through their art, music, dance, words, and other outlets. The
enemy doesn't want this reflection of God so prominently displayed, so he whispers:

Look at them. You could never be as good as them.

See? Nobody needs your art!

Everything good has already been created.

These lies create an envious spirit toward those who are doing
something you've claimed as yours. Envy is all about stopping
you from moving forward and keeping you locked into thoughts
such as, *How dare they be (fill in the blank).*

This type of self-pity and envy is sin, and it's important for us to call it that instead of embracing the lie that we are unable to create anything of value on our own. If God wants you to create, then what He has asked you to do deserves your obedience, without wondering if someone else has already done it or could do it better. This request from God makes us feel vulnerable; He is asking us to obey Him even when we doubt. But it's honoring to Him when we use our creative gifts, despite Satan's lies.

SHIFT IN FOCUS

Where do you need to name envy in your life?

Take a moment and pray for conviction in this area and freedom from Satan's lies. If these words reflect your heart, please borrow them:

Dear heavenly Father, I'm sorry for the times I've listened to Satan's lies over Your truth. Envy has been a chain I've been lugging behind me for a long time, and I want to be free. Please give me this freedom and empower me to turn to You instead of pitying myself. Please convict me of the envy in my life that I have yet to name and set me free, in Your name. Amen.

● ● ● ● ● ● ● ● ● ● ● ● **DAY 14**

Envy in Relationships

> *Love is patient and kind; love does not envy or boast;*
> *it is not arrogant.*
> (1 Corinthians 13:4)

Fours experience a lot of envy in relationships for two main reasons:

1. You feel you are lacking. You may fear that even if you do gain a friendship, that friend will eventually find a better friend than you, or simply find you are *not enough*. This may cause you to push the person away in order to see if they are *really* loyal to you. You may refuse to initiate contact or simply ignore them for a couple of days, especially as you start to feel emotionally invested in the friendship.

2. You go to type Two in stress (more on this later), which puts a spotlight on all the ways in which your relationships are lacking, causing a deep sense of pain. We envy those we perceive as having the relationships, and we despair that we have to *be enough* in order to *earn* the love we crave. This despairing panic can cause you to *pull in* people, bringing them closer to you and showering them with gifts, attention, trips—anything you feel will make them value you and your friendship more.

We must remember the verse above about what *love* looks like, even as we experience envy in our relationships. Love does *not* envy. What does that look like? It looks like seeing your friend, spouse, or family member enjoying someone else's company and, instead of feeling threatened, choosing to be happy for them.

I struggled with this a lot early in my marriage as my husband, who used to be so excited to see me, slowly shifted to being more outwardly excited to see his family. This was so upsetting; it felt like a betrayal. I was envious of his family and the part of him that used to be just for me.

As our first year of marriage flew by, I began to see my hurt for what it was—sin. And I saw his joy for what it was—beautiful. His joy in seeing his family wasn't taking anything away from me; it was a gift to them. This realization has helped me love my husband, and his family, in a much better way than by trying to demand the sole attention he once gave me, or worse, to demand that he not act excited to see his family.

So, even when envy feels justified and everything seems unfair, consider love, dear Four. Love does not envy.

SHIFT IN FOCUS

What would it mean to love your friend, family, or spouse by not envying? Is this a part of your life that needs change and repentance?

• • • • • • • • • • • DAY 15

Envy in Creative Expression

Let us not become conceited, provoking one another,
envying one another.
(Galatians 5:26)

Okay, Fours, are you ready for some more tough love? Today, we are talking about envy in our creative expressions. Creative expression is one of the amazing ways we get to reflect our creator God, and it takes *so* many forms. However, Fours are notorious for self-sabotaging, starting new things before they finish their last *best idea*, and just giving up.

Why? I'd like to suggest that a big culprit is *envy*.

Envy taps you on the shoulder and says:

"You'll never be as good as them."

"Why try when you can't be the best at this?

"You might as well stop now before you're too invested."

These whispers are lies from the enemy, sent to distract you from your purpose and the God-glorifying gifts in your life.

No matter how uncontrollable your envy may feel, or how discouraged you may get, God is bigger than all of it. God can help, and He has good works that need your attention, whether you feel motivated or not.

> *For we are his workmanship, created in Christ Jesus for good works, which God prepared beforehand, that we should walk in them.* (Ephesians 2:10)

Trust Him by taking that step.

Maybe it comes in the form of unfollowing someone on social media. You don't need to play the hero and fight envy every time they show up in your feed.

Maybe it's going back and finishing a half-completed project.

Maybe it's texting that friend who took up the same hobby as you, and then things got weird.

Maybe it's asking for help.

Ask God to help you see what your next step is.

SHIFT IN FOCUS

What would it look like if you pushed through the lies? What might you have accomplished by now for God's kingdom?

Who do you struggle with envying every time they show up on your newsfeed? What would it look like if you unfollowed your competition on social media?

What would it look like if you prioritized your creative expression?

• • • • • • • • • • • • **DAY 16**

How to Spot an Envious Thought

A tranquil heart gives life to the flesh, but envy makes the bones rot.
(Proverbs 14:30)

The biggest gift learning about the Enneagram has given me is realizing my propensity toward envy. Maybe that's a weird statement, but it's true nonetheless.

Envy used to have such a claim on my heart that I would even stress about seeing people I *might* have cause to envy. I envied other girls' bodies. I envied attention loved ones would give other people. I envied talent. I envied success. I envied extroverts. I envied blondes.

There really were no boundaries for that sick feeling that would settle into my thoughts and cause all sorts of emotional distress. The weird thing is that I never would have called it *envy*. I thought it was just self-pity or being judgmental. I believed it was the lives of other people victimizing me!

I would think, *How dare extroverts exist! How dare they show up and be extroverted when I don't have a chance to compete. They shouldn't be allowed here.*

To me, these were just judgmental thoughts, but they were hiding a dark and vulnerable secret: I was jealous. My *Introvert and Proud* bumper sticker might beg to differ, but God knew the truth.

Once I came to terms with my envy, I wasn't able to hide behind secondary motives anymore. The more I name *envy* in my thoughts and emotions, the less power it has over me, and this is the freedom I want for you too.

Dear Four, can you spot an envious thought? Maybe yes, but maybe your envy is still hiding. If so, here's a formula you can follow.

Just follow the bread crumbs.

What's causing you to feel anger or self-pity? Extroverts.

Why is this causing you to feel this way? They make you feel *less than.*

Why? Because they steal all the likability in the room.

Why? Because they're good at social stuff.

And why does this bother you? Because I'm not good at this social stuff.

Is this envy? Yes.

SHIFT IN FOCUS

Take a moment to think about a recent sick feeling of envy and follow the bread crumbs of your thoughts and feelings:

What's causing you to feel anger or self-pity?

Why are you feeling this way?

Is this envy?

If you have come to the conclusion that this recent feeling was envy, repent and thank God for exposing the *rotting in your bones.*

If it's not, try to think about someone in your life whom you've always disliked or resented. Could envy be the root problem?

• • • • • • • • • • • • DAY 17

Scarcity vs. Abundance

The thief comes only to steal and kill and destroy. I came that they may have life and have it abundantly.
(John 10:10)

Have you ever heard of a scarcity mindset? It goes something like this:

Life is like a pie, and when someone else is given a big piece, there is less for you.

The opposite of this is an abundance mindset. It looks like this:

Life is like Thanksgiving dinner. When everyone is eating, everyone is happy. Everyone brought something to share. There are always leftovers, so eat your fill. Sharing and thankfulness abound.

Most of us go through life with a scarcity mindset, especially those of us who struggle with envy. It always seems as though someone who is undeserving has more than we do, so we easily get stuck in the trap of anger and self-pity regarding our circumstances. Shifting into an abundance mindset is not only biblical, it's also healthier for you. It brings freedom from envy.

God's love is described by the Greek word *agape*, which means never-ending, bigger than life, unstoppable love. God loving others, and even blessing them, has nothing to do with what is left over for you.

There is enough for everyone, but there is also a different plan for everyone. A blessing for one person may be a curse to another person. Thankfully, we don't get to decide these things. There is so much freedom to be found in thinking abundantly. Scarcity thinking means you're always looking to the right or left, measuring their slice of pie and comparing it to your own. In other words, scarcity thinking is exhausting.

Jesus came to give us life abundantly, and it doesn't stop there. We get to enjoy this abundant life with Him for eternity. So, what would it look like for you to think bigger and enjoy life like it's an unending Thanksgiving dinner instead of a single, measly pie?

SHIFT IN FOCUS

Who in your life has a big piece of the pie?

How would your feelings toward them change if you were able to think more abundantly?

● ● ● ● ● ● ● ● ● ● ● DAY 18

Growing in an Abundance Mindset
By Christine Rollings

> *Rejoice always, pray without ceasing, give thanks in all*
> *circumstances; for this is the will of God in Christ Jesus for you.*
> (1 Thessalonians 5:16–18)

Having an abundance mindset isn't the most natural thing for us to do. It's so easy to look around and keep account of what we're lacking. The world around us reinforces this. Want more money? You better hustle. Want to find a partner? Put yourself out there. Want better mental health? That self-care is on you, baby.

And while there is truth in all of these things, the focus on *more* and *better* isn't what the abundance mindset is all about. We're not preparing for that Thanksgiving dinner; we're already there!

It takes work and time to train ourselves to think this way. In her book, *One Thousand Gifts*, Ann Voskamp writes, "Practice is the hardest part of learning, and training is the essence of transformation."[3] So how do we train ourselves to see the abundance of the feast before us? Paul tells us in his first letter to the Thessalonians!

"Rejoice always..."

"Pray without ceasing..."

"Give thanks in all circumstances."

---

3. Ann Voskamp, *One Thousand Gifts: A Dare to Live Fully Right Where You Are* (Grand Rapids, MI: Zondervan, 2012).

We should give thanks in *all things*, whether we feel like we are lacking or not, whether we feel like we're getting the last or the biggest piece of pie or not. When we feel like others have it better than we do, or we feel like we have a lot to measure up to, even then, we are to rejoice and give thanks.

We can acknowledge the anger and envy. We can name it and call it out for what it is, and *also* name the things around us that remind us that we have enough.

You can say, "I am envious of extroverts because I'm not good at this social stuff," and *also* say, "I am grateful for my close friends and the conversations that we have."

Over time, with practice and prayer, we can grow in gratitude for the abundance before us, leaning into the truth that there is more than enough for us all.

SHIFT IN FOCUS

Let the training begin! Today, make a list of three things you are thankful for. Write them in your journal, on your phone, or here on this page. Make this a daily habit for this whole week. Decide to do it when you first wake up or before you go to bed.

I'm grateful for:

	Day 1	Day 2	Day 3	Day 4	Day 5	Day 6	Day 7
#1							
#2							
#3							

• • • • • • • • • • • **DAY 19**

Elizabeth's Abundance Mindset
By Christine Rollings

And blessed is she who believed that there would be a fulfillment of
what was spoken to her from the Lord.
(Luke 1:45)

Remember the Christmas story in the book of Luke? Right there, between the angel Gabriel announcing Jesus's birth to Mary and Mary singing her song of praise to the Lord, is a part of the story that we often read past quickly. It goes like this: Mary goes to visit her cousin Elizabeth, who is also pregnant. I can imagine the Instagram post: "So glad I get to be pregnant at the same time as my cousin! #futurebesties"

Upon hearing Mary's voice, the baby inside Elizabeth leaps! In their celebration, Elizabeth is the first person to verbally confirm what Mary heard from the angel. She says, *"Blessed are you among women, and blessed is the fruit of your womb! And why is this granted to me that the mother of my Lord should come to me?"* (Luke 1:42–43).

Elizabeth is filled with pure gratitude. She names what is true: Mary is blessed, and so is her child.

Elizabeth could so easily have been overcome by envy.

Earlier in the opening paragraphs of Luke, we learn of Elizabeth and her husband, Zechariah. Both were righteous and blameless, *"but they had no child, because Elizabeth was barren, and both were advanced in years"* (verse 7).

Elizabeth was infertile. I can imagine the years of trying and the months of disappointment, longing, and heartache. Finally, in her old age, God has promised her a son—a special son who *"will be great before the Lord"* (verse 15). Her joy was immense!

Then her young, unwed cousin comes to visit—and she's pregnant with a *very* special son, the Son of God Himself.

If Elizabeth was an unhealthy Four, I imagine her saying something like this: "It's so easy for her; she doesn't know my years of heartache and longing! I thought I was special to the Lord, but He obviously counts my cousin as more special than me."

But that isn't what Elizabeth said and not what she believed. Her words were rooted in a heart overflowing with love for God, for her cousin, and both of these tiny babies. Her response isn't envy but gratitude. She expresses gratitude that she would get to be even some small part of this greater story! Elizabeth isn't lamenting Mary's bigger piece of pie; she's celebrating that they get to be at the table together, partaking of God's abundant blessing.

SHIFT IN FOCUS

Read the first chapter of Luke on your own.

How would you have responded if you were Elizabeth?

Now, imagine yourself responding as Elizabeth did. What would have to be true of your heart for that to happen freely?

• • • • • • • • • • • DAY 20

Defeating Envy in Your Life

Search me, O God, and know my heart!
Try me and know my thoughts!
(Psalm 139:23)

After nine days of focusing on envy, you may be feeling a little hopeless. You may be at the point of seeing the problem but feeling very weak in the fight. We've all been there.

Can I be honest with you? We are all weak; we can't defeat envy on our own, and you don't have to.

We hear a lot of good, practical advice, but it can often simply be seen as "pulling yourself up by your bootstraps and getting over the problem." No matter how practical the advice, the power to change comes from Christ, not by our own strength.

Noticing your envy and seeing it as sin is the first step toward surrender, and toward running into your Father's arms, hands dirty and asking for help. Every time you think abundantly instead of with scarcity, you give glory to Him. Every time you love instead of envy, you give glory to Him. It is the changing and sanctifying work of the Holy Spirit that will change this in you, not your own strength, not this devotional, and not a loyal friend. It's God, and God alone, who can break these chains.

This change in your heart may appear as noticing an envious thought, repenting to God immediately, and asking Him to help you think in abundance.

This change may appear as asking God to search your heart and show you all the places you can't see where envy is impacting you.

This change may appear as loving someone well, even when your heart doesn't feel like it.

As much as our envy may feel justified and out of our control, this change is something we long for, isn't it? Envy is gross, painful, and devastating. As justified as it may seem in the moment, it only leads to heartache and loneliness. So, as you desire this change, ask God for it!

> *Ask, and it will be given to you; seek, and you will find; knock, and it will be opened to you. For everyone who asks receives, and the one who seeks finds, and to the one who knocks it will be opened. Or which one of you, if his son asks him for bread, will give him a stone? Or if he asks for a fish, will give him a serpent? If you then, who are evil, know how to give good gifts to your children, how much more will your Father who is in heaven give good things to those who ask him!* (Matthew 7:7–11)

SHIFT IN FOCUS

Will you pause with me and pray this prayer?

Dear heavenly Father, I repent that my heart is prone to envy. This feeling has plagued me for longer than I can remember, and I almost can't imagine my life without its bitter sting. I know that this envy is a sin, and I'm sorry that I have sinned against You and others by indulging it. Please change my heart, and help me to flee from the temptation to envy. I need Your comfort, Your peace, and Your strength, Lord God. I thank You that You are my ever-present help in times of trouble. Amen.

10 Days of Being a Space Saver
Your Strength and How To Use It

• • • • • • • • • • • **DAY 21**

What Is Space Saving?

Bear one another's burdens, and so fulfill the law of Christ.
(Galatians 6:2)

Have you ever been running late to an event, and as you parked, you wondered if there would even be a seat for you inside? Would you be sitting alone? Or with someone you don't know? I know I've had these thoughts and have almost turned around and gone home as the result. How would you feel if, instead of having to sit at an empty corner table, a friend waved you over? They saved a seat for you right next to them.

Consideration, a flooding relief, a smile. This is a good feeling, a good moment.

Now, if we can turn this situation into a strictly emotional one, you are halfway to understanding one of the biggest giftings of type Fours—space saving. This isn't in the literal sense of saving chairs, booths, or theater seats, but as Fours, we provide emotional space for others to process, grieve, and feel what they're feeling.

As Fours, we bring nonjudgmental space for others to process and explore their own emotions, especially hard ones. We aren't scared of emotional expression, we aren't taken aback that they feel such things, and we are emotionally open enough to dive into the depths of feelings with them. This is a gift.

One of your friends might be thinking right now, *Will there be space for me? Will I be alone? Will I be processing this with a stranger in therapy years from now?* It is Fours' *happy place* to answer this call. "We have space for you; you don't need to be alone; I won't judge or leave you."

Sometimes people need to vent everything, just to have you digest it and repeat it back to them. Sometimes people need you to ask questions. Sometimes your friend may just need to cry with someone safe. These things show you're listening and you care. Have you been this person? My gut tells me you have.

This is space saving in its simplest and purest form, and although it might not always feel like a gift to you, it's invaluable to others to have someone there when it really counts.

SHIFT IN FOCUS

Reflect on your last year. Who have you been a space saver for? What are their names?

Write them here:

| |
| |
| |
| |
| |

Take a moment, while they're on your mind, to pray for them. Thank God for sharing His compassionate heart through you.

• • • • • • • • • • • **DAY 22**

Our Space-Saving God

> *He was despised and rejected by men, a man of sorrows and*
> *acquainted with grief.*
> (Isaiah 53:3)

As we talk about this concept of space saving, we can't help but empathize with our perfect space-saving God.

In the book of Psalms, we see David process his emotions. God gave David space in His own holy Word to do that. If that doesn't tell you how important emotions are to God, I don't know what does. David's emotions (fear, guilt, joy) all lead him to the feet of the Lord in worship. This is what our emotions do when we process them with our space-saving God. He can not only handle your emotions, but He cares about them. When you're walking with God, emotions, creative expression, tears, pain, and joy can all ultimately lead you into a closer relationship with Him.

A person who is gifted with space saving feels safe to be around. They don't try to fix you, they may cry with you, and they check back in. These are the marks of a space saver. God does this with us. He is safe. He feels with you. He doesn't forget you, and He doesn't need you to get yourself together before you come to Him.

When we look at Isaiah 53:3, we see that Jesus was well acquainted with emotions, both good and bad. Jesus understands what you're going through, He has felt the spectrum of human emotion, and He is now at the right hand of God advocating and praying for you.

God is not only our ultimate space-saving example, He's the space saver for the space savers. When no one else feels safe, or you wish someone would listen, He's waiting with an eager ear. He loves you, and He has all the space in the world for you.

SHIFT IN FOCUS

Dear Heavenly Father, I thank You for making me a space saver for others, and that You are the ultimate space saver for us. I know I need to run into Your arms more often, and let You turn my angst into joy. Thank You for the times You've wept with me, prayed for me, and laughed with me. I'm in awe of Your love for me. Amen.

• • • • • • • • • • • DAY 23

Coming Beside Others in Tenderness

Behold, we consider those blessed who remained steadfast. You have heard of the steadfastness of Job, and you have seen the purpose of the Lord, how the Lord is compassionate and merciful.
(James 5:11)

In tenderness He sought me,
Weary and sick with sin,
And on His shoulders brought me
Back to His fold again.[4]

I love the hymn "In Tenderness He Sought Me." If you have a moment to listen, you can find it on YouTube, or wherever you listen to music. It's a great song, a beautiful picture of the gospel and our tender Savior.

I mention this song because tenderness, which can mean a sensitivity to pain, is something Fours are especially gifted in. Being naturally attuned to our own emotions seeps out into this empathy and intuition about others emotional well-being. We can read emotions, faces, and body language. When we are healthy, we react with empathy, compassion, and space for that person to feel what they need to feel.

Easy, gentle, kind ... this is what tenderness means. Fours tenderly come alongside those who are hurting and bear witness to their pain. We listen, we support, we empathize, but most

4. W. Spencer Walton, "In Tenderness He Sought Me" (1894).

importantly, we don't shy away. We don't try to fix; we just show up. We don't need them to stop; we just need them to be honest about what's going on inside.

This may feel natural to you, but I assure you it's a gifting that not many people have. It's natural for people to shy away from pain, to not know what to do, to try to fix what seems broken, or to try to make others' pain stop, but for Fours, it's so much more than that. It's about a heart, and it's about healing. Wounds need time to heal, and no one knows that more than Fours do. We've watched the process, we have our own scars, and most of us would count ourselves experts in the pains of life.

SHIFT IN FOCUS

Can you think of a visual picture for tenderness? Think of a mom stroking her baby's cheek, or a dad teaching his little boy to play the sport he loves.

If you are so artistically inclined, draw a picture of what tenderness looks like to you.

• • • • • • • • • • • DAY 24

A Non-Judgmental Heart

Judge not, that you be not judged. For with the judgment you
pronounce you will be judged, and with the measure you use it
will be measured to you. Why do you see the speck that is in your
brother's eye, but do not notice the log that is in your own eye? Or
how can you say to your brother, 'Let me take the speck out of your
eye,' when there is the log in your own eye? You hypocrite, first take
the log out of your own eye, and then you will see clearly to take the
speck out of your brother's eye.
(Matthew 7:1–5)

I am an Enneagram coach, which is a lot like being a life coach. My clients often apologize for the things they tell me.

"It's horrible that I just admitted that; I'm sorry." "I'm sorry I'm just unloading on you; you probably don't want to know all of this."

"I'm telling you too much; I'm sorry."

"Oh no, I can't believe I said that out loud. You must think I'm a horrible person."

When this happens, I explain a simple fact: "I'm a Four, which means I have a fairly nonjudgmental heart. I am possibly the most messed-up person on this phone call, so I don't really care what you've done, as long as you're being honest. Usually, the more difficult it is to admit, the more I can tell you are being honest. This might sound odd, but what you just shared makes me want to stand up and clap, because you're being authentic. Admitting there is a problem is a great first step to the self-awareness of what's going on inside you. Most people aren't brave enough to do that, and I am proud of you."

A truth about Fours you may not realize is that we don't often stand back or gasp when others are baring their hearts to us. We actually feel a sense of honor to be taken into their confidence. We love deep, no-fluff conversations, and we have a naturally nonjudgmental heart in these situations.

If our hearts ever appear to be judgmental, this is often envy in disguise. Dear Four, if we take a good look at your heart, and the authentic things people have spoken to you, I believe it would be hard to find a speck of judgment. Hurt, surprise, or sadness, yes, but not usually stone-cold judgment.

Dear Four, the times you've sensed yourself slipping into judgment, it's probably because you felt manipulated, or believed that the other party was lying to you.

Now, when someone honestly admits something that hurts you, you may be angry at first, but when the dust settles, you'll feel relieved to be talking about the problem. Nothing is worse than the feeling of distance in a relationship, and although hard truths hurt, they yield thoughtful conversations and the possibility of a deeper connection.

SHIFT IN FOCUS

Dear Four, do you recognize your own nonjudgmental heart in these words? There is nothing broken or missing about you.

You were created complete, and on purpose. Just the way you are. You nonjudgmental heart is a huge picture of that truth.

Take a moment to write a thank-you note to your heart for how it nonjudgmentally keeps space for others. End the note with giving glory to God for blessing you with this gift.

DAY 25 • • • • • • • • • • • •

Empathy
By Alison Bradley

Rejoice with those who rejoice, weep with those who weep.
(Romans 12:15)
Be kind to one another, tenderhearted.
(Ephesians 4:32)

As someone who repressed her emotions for years, I'm tremendously grateful for the Fours in my life and their gift of empathy. They have been a safe space for me to feel and express my emotions, inviting me to listen to the message they hold. It might be hard for Fours to understand, since feeling emotions is one of your superpowers, but I've struggled to create space for my own emotions in the past. As I've grown in this, it has been a tremendous gift to have the Fours in my life show me empathy.

I remember times in the last few years when I began to cry during a small group meeting while sharing something tender and personal. I couldn't help but notice the responses to my vulnerability. Some people shifted in their seats, made visibly uncomfortable by my raw emotions. However, the Four in the room smiled and quickly leaned in. Her smile wasn't a celebration of my pain, but a celebration of my courage to show up here. She asked helpful questions about my experience, inviting me to go deeper and share more. I felt her compassion and empathy, as she listened and created space for me.

When I experience a Four's empathy, I'm offered more than just a safe space to experience my emotions. I'm celebrated for the courage to listen to reality. I'm invited to be curious and gentle with myself as I listen to what my emotions have to say to me. I believe this is a beautiful picture of what the Lord asks us to offer to each other, loving in this way as we were first loved by Him.

SHIFT IN FOCUS

Pause to read these verses from 1 John 4 as you reflect on the way the Lord has gifted you with empathy as a tool to love others:

> *Beloved, let us love one another, for love is from God, and whoever loves has been born of God and knows God. … In this the love of God was made manifest among us, that God sent his only Son into the world, so that we might live through him. In this is love, not that we have loved God but that he loved us and sent his Son to be the propitiation for our sins. Beloved, if God so loved us, we also ought to love one another. No one has ever seen God; if we love one another, God abides in us and his love is perfected in us.*
>
> (1 John 4:7, 9–12)

You get to reflect the love of God to others through your gift of empathy. This passage preaches the truth that it is not because we are lovely or full of love that God loves us. He offers us His love, not seeking to fix us but to offer freedom from sin and death. This is the kind of love you offer to those around you, not seeking to fix them but to offer the freedom of being loved in the midst of their hardships.

Pause to thank God for His love for you, and the way you get to reflect that love to others.

DAY 26 • • • • • • • • • • • •

A Heart Battered by Shame

But the Lord God helps me; therefore I have not been disgraced;
therefore I have set my face like a flint,
and I know that I shall not be put to shame.
(Isaiah 50:7)

One of the reasons Fours are especially sensitive and empathetic towards the pain of others is because we are no strangers to pain. Not only are our emotions loud and in our face, we also have an inner-shamer, thanks to being in the heart triad, that tells us horrible things about our worth. We think, *You'll never be enough. Why even try?*

When you've been hit over the head with shame your whole life, you need the utmost gentleness from other people. This is why Fours are often called overly sensitive. Some people point out the weaknesses that our inner-shamer has already told us, so we react with more pain and shame. We get defensive, or what others label *too sensitive*.

Unfortunately, this has been the reaction from a lot of well-meaning people toward us for our entire life. We were in pain and didn't need to be *fixed*, just heard. Instead we got what sounded like more shame. We needed a gentle touch from others to help us believe that what the inner-shamer was saying wasn't true, but alas this is not what we received. So we proceed forward with trying to give the gentleness we need to others. I'm sure you can't imagine approaching someone else's pain any other way.

We know that shame is loud, and the last thing a hurting person needs is to feel like we are *too sensitive*, or a *burden*, or that something is wrong with them. They need empathy, gentleness, space, a hug—and someone to tell them they're not crazy or wrong for feeling how they're feeling.

Shame may be a burden, but just like God does with so many things, what Satan meant for evil, God uses for good. Our hearts may be battered by shame, but consequently, our hands are full of grace.

SHIFT IN FOCUS

What is one good thing that has come out of your heart being battered by shame?

We could spend this time listing the people who have hurt us, but it's much more productive and healthier to give thanks for what God has done with that pain. Amen!

DAY 27 • • • • • • • • • • •

Honoring Emotions

Blessed are those who mourn, for they shall be comforted.
(Matthew 5:4)

Picture the last time you felt like you might die from a broken heart. … Got it? Now why were you feeling this way?

For me, I can clearly remember the moment I was told that my baby had died in my womb. The world stopped, and my heart was left shattered on the ground. I never wasted one moment feeling guilty for being sad about my miscarriage. The reason I was sad was worth every moment of my grief, no matter how painful.

Fours feel an innate sense of respect toward emotions, particularly sadness. It feels disrespectful—to the situation, to ourselves, even to God—to not fully feel what is born in our hearts.

This respect for emotions and grief sometimes gives us a sober mindset toward the world, but it is extremely helpful to those who feel guilty for taking time to grieve to have a sympathetic Four in their life. Our culture is quick to grieve, quick to move on, and always on the go. This produces a short shelf life for grief. If someone dies, you get a couple of days to grieve, maybe a couple of weeks, but then you'll hear these comments:

"Are you feeling better?"

"I know that was horrible but…"

"You know you can look on the bright side."

"Choose joy!"

If you're truly honoring your grief, these comments feel disrespectful toward the source of your pain. My baby's life was not *only worth* a couple days of tears. I will be grieving my daughter's life, in one way or another, until I meet her in heaven. That's how much she matters. If God cared enough to create her, she deserves to be remembered, and my grief over her life has no shelf life. Maybe you feel the same about the last time your heart felt the sting of a devastating loss.

This natural instinct of honoring emotions makes us invaluable to the hurting. This is why many Fours are pastors, counselors, and caregivers. We are good at honoring what needs to be grieved, and not rushing the process for others.

SHIFT IN FOCUS

Has your natural respect for emotions ever made you feel weird, or defective?

"The LORD is near to the brokenhearted and saves the crushed in spirit" (Psalm 34:18). God comes alongside us and gives us the space to grieve. He doesn't set a timer; He's not judging you. In fact, He may be weeping with you, and He's not leaving anytime soon. This is comfort, and this is what God freely offers your broken heart. Don't let the world make you feel any differently.

DAY 28 • • • • • • • • • • •

Even When You Don't Feel Helpful
By Alison Bradley

Come, see a man who told me all that I ever did. Can this be the Christ?
(John 4:29)

Your gift as a space saver is just that: a gift. It can be challenging when you can't control what someone does with the gift you offer them. For someone who is ready to deeply engage in their own growth process, your strength will be a gift they are grateful to receive. But for someone who is not ready, this gift may not be appreciated. Even though you've created a space for someone else's emotions, they might not be ready or willing to enter into that place with you.

This person might be visibly uncomfortable or continually change the subject. They may avoid talking to you, especially if they know you well enough to know that their heart might be exposed during your time together. Dear Four, please hear that this may not have anything to do with you.

When your gift is not received the way you hoped, it can be confusing and hurtful. It is always wise to check in with the Lord about your own heart condition when someone pulls away, but someone refusing your gift may not be a reflection on you at all. The other person might still be growing in their process of dealing with anger or grief. You may be tempted to take this rejection personally, but the Lord can help you see your gift for what it is: something offered that is separate from you.

If you have a few moments, pause and read the account of Jesus with the woman of Samaria in John 4:7–42. Notice the Samaritan woman's initial responses to Jesus. At first, she's fairly unreceptive to Him being a space saver for her. She avoids His invitation to speak about deep things and changes the subject. Notice that Jesus continues to invite her to grow and to deeper, personal conversation. But He allows this to be her choice, as He creates space for her and her story. In the end, she chooses to accept the gift of this exposure of her reality.

Notice that what the woman says in verse 29 is repeated in verse 39: *"He told me all that I ever did."*

There is no shame in what she tells others at the end of her encounter with the Lord; she realizes that Jesus isn't exposing her to humiliate her. With Jesus, the exposure of our hearts, our motivations, our secret thoughts, and our emotions does not bring shame. Jesus brings things into the light with an invitation, just as He offered the Samaritan woman: to be loved just as you are, and to repent if needed. And you, dear Four, offer others the same kind of space to be seen and loved. This is true whether or not it is received as the gift that it is.

SHIFT IN FOCUS

Pause to ask the Lord to help you see your space saving as a gift. He knows what it is like to have others be unreceptive to what He has to offer. Ask Jesus to help you hold tight to truth when you feel rejected as a space saver. He can help you have patience and grace. Ask the Lord to use you and your gift for His glory, as you seek to partner with Him to bring His kingdom to those around you.

DAY 29 • • • • • • • • • • •

When Others Won't Save Space for You

See to it that no one fails to obtain the grace of God; that no "root of bitterness" springs up and causes trouble.
(Hebrews 12:15)

If we aren't careful, bitterness and resentment can build up in our hearts because of the times we didn't have anyone to save space for us. With every personality type, the things we are most gifted in ourselves are the areas that cause us the most pain when not received from others. Because space saving is so natural for us, we can't imagine not doing this for others, and it feels like rejection to us when others withhold it.

Please know, dear Four, that this has nothing to do with you. Others' reactions to you have so much more to do with what's going on inside of them than what they're receiving from you. Emotions like sadness and grief make others uncomfortable, even anxious. It can be selfish; they often want to leave feeling that they fixed something for you. They want a sense of accomplishment. Or they don't want to have to deal with you in the same state again. They might be in a season in which they are just not the best space saver. They don't have the room or the emotional energy to sit with others in their pain, and that's not sinful or bad. This is why we need more than one person to go to when the storm comes. Even *you* are not always in the best place to space save.

Our reaction to people who reject our gift is our responsibility, and it's the only thing we can control. The healthiest, and most godly stance towards those who neglect or hurt us is to have compassion for them. This doesn't mean you keep giving and giving your gift as a space saver with them when they've proven that they can't handle it, but it's a posture of grace. They aren't gifted in the same area that we are, and that's okay.

You don't need to have your burdens bared before you can start helping others, and your heart is likely drawing you towards this conclusion. Jesus is our ultimate example of this, and I'm sure no one on earth space saved for Him like He did for others. Aren't we glad He didn't wait?

As we mentioned earlier, many Fours are in ministry, counseling, and caregiving careers, all of which call for space saving. There is something in your heart that knows you're good at this, and you want to help. Don't let bitterness derail this call.

SHIFT IN FOCUS

Let God help your heart forgive, and walk in grace toward people who have not space saved for you. What names do you need to fill in here?

_____ is not good at space saving for me, and that's okay.

_____ has not responded to me in my time of need, like I would have for them. I need to forgive them.

I am gifted at space saving, and I can see this gifting in myself when I _____.

DAY 30 • • • • • • • • • • • •

Living With Your Arms Open

You keep him in perfect peace whose mind is stayed on you,
because he trusts in you. Trust in the LORD forever,
for the LORD GOD is an everlasting rock.
(Isaiah 26:3–4)

When God is our stability, our comfort, and our rock, little can derail our fixed gaze on Him. I want to live like this, and I'm sure you do too. The problem is we live in a fallen world; we are sinful people, and though fixation on God is our heart's desire, our flesh wars against it. We fail, we let go, we get distracted, we act out, and we sin, but God is still here with open arms. How beautiful is that?

As we space save for others, and deal with the pain of others not space saving for us, may we trust God. May we go to Him and trust Him.

He will put people in your arms to comfort, and He will rip other people away. May we trust Him.

He will bless us, and He will be there in the storm. May we trust Him.

He will lift us up, and He will humble us. May we trust Him.

He will fill your heart, and He will empty it. May we trust Him.

He will give you good days, and He will be with you in bad days. May we trust Him.

He made us space savers, and He made us filled to the brim with emotion. May we trust Him.

He created us, and He numbered our days. May we trust Him, and glorify Him with our lives.

SHIFT IN FOCUS

What do you need to trust God with today? Where in your life do you need His hand?

Are you struggling to live with your arms open to what He will give you because He might also take it away?

Trust in the LORD with all your heart, and do not lean on your own understanding. In all your ways acknowledge him, and he will make straight your paths.   (Proverbs 3:5–6)

10 Days of Letting Go of Self-Absorption

A Common Pain Point

• • • • • • • • • • • DAY 31

Why Do Fours Have a Reputation of Being Self-Absorbed?

Do nothing from selfish ambition or conceit, but in humility count others more significant than yourselves. Let each of you look not only to his own interests, but also to the interests of others.
(Philippians 2:3–4)

Fours being *self-absorbed* is a pretty common stereotype. It's one that is both accurate and hurtful, so I want to tread lightly. Just know that I'm talking about myself here; I have firsthand experience dealing with this pain point.

Fours have an internal spotlight, and their focus is on emotions. When we are *healthy* this spotlight looks like empathy and self-awareness. We are able to spotlight others' emotions, space save for them, and help them process what's going on in their heart. We also have a good read on what *we* are personally feeling. We know which feelings are valid and there for a purpose and which emotions need to be disregarded.

When we are *average* in health, it seems like we're flip-flopping between focusing too much on ourselves and too much on others. We might dip into health sometimes and experience the gift that this internal spotlight is, but most of the time, it feels exhausting to be so aware.

When we are *unhealthy*, our spotlight shines inward. Every emotion takes center stage in our thoughts long after the applause has quieted. When our spotlight is stuck on self, this is when we are self-absorbed. Literally all of our energy is going towards how *everything* is making us feel. This is so exhausting. But spotlighting every feeling without a filter feel justified when others have disregarded our important emotions in the past or continue to do so. Suddenly, how we feel becomes all-important.

This is not a godly way to emote and isn't using any of the talents the Lord gave you to help others. It also feels miserable! You're literally a slave to your own emotions, and they're a very fickle master.

Over the next nine days, we'll be looking at this internal spotlight, how it functions, how it looks to others, and what it means to feel emotions in a godly way.

SHIFT IN FOCUS

What level of health do you feel like you're in right now? Healthy, average, or unhealthy?

• • • • • • • • • • • DAY 32

How Does This Feel from the Inside?

*Whoever sings songs to a heavy heart is like one who
takes off a garment on a cold day.*
(Proverbs 25:20)

Living with an *emotional spotlight* feels like something is wrong with you. While many people can stick their emotional responses on a back burner, for Fours, everything hits the windshield. We *can't* ignore whatever strong emotional response is taking center stage for us at the moment. There's no *choose joy* quote or positive affirmation that makes our emotions go away; they have to be worked through, and it *is* work! A sign of health in Fours is our ability to filter and process these emotions, not whether or not we have them, or if we can shove them away.

As a Four, you may have had parents who tried to help you to shove your emotions away; after all, this is how they dealt with strong emotions. However, this can increase a young Four's feeling of brokenness, which makes it harder to process emotions as an adult who really would like to not feel everything so strongly.

The good news is that if you talk to any counselor, they'll tell you that facing your emotions is the healthiest way to deal with them. Shoving emotions away is not good for you, even if it feels more pleasant in the moment. Just like growing pains, or childbirth, the pain has a purpose. With Fours, it keeps us more emotionally aware, and can help us process and heal faster than others, even if we don't see this right away.

SHIFT IN FOCUS

You probably don't verbalize this or think it's different from others, but you currently have tools you use to process emotions.

Do you ever just go for a drive with no destination in mind? Do you turn up the music? Do you dive into creating? Do you talk to your significant other? Do you have a good cry? Do you spend time in nature? What do *you* do?

I _____ and _____
to help me process my strong emotions.

The likelihood is that you are coping, because we all have to do that. If you can't think of a way that you're coping successfully, feel free to try out some of the things I just mentioned. Music can be especially good medicine for any emotion.

● ● ● ● ● ● ● ● ● ● ● **DAY 33**

How Does This Look from the Outside?

> *For the LORD sees not as man sees: man looks on the outward*
> *appearance, but the LORD looks on the heart.*
> (1 Samuel 16:7)

Fours are different from other people. Of course, we are *all* different from each other; that's one of the reasons the Enneagram is so helpful! However, being different for a Four is both lonely and satisfying in a way that is hard to explain.

The thing is, we feel that others find us complicated and that they try to simplify our feelings. When we are *unhealthy*, this is what other Enneagram types might think about our spotlight on emotion:

Type Ones: *They don't seem to have any self-control.*

Type Twos: *They're too focused on themselves and need to be more sacrificial.*

Type Threes: *They can't get anything done when they're so stuck in the past.*

Type Fours: *They think about themselves a lot. My emotions are important too.*

Type Fives: *I don't know how they have enough energy to think about their emotions so much.*

Type Sixes: *Little things seem to be a big deal to them.*

Type Sevens: *Honestly, they're kind of a mood kill.*

Type Eights: *They're too sensitive.*

Type Nines: *They're kind of exhausting.*

These are all things other Enneagram types—yes, including healthy Fours—have said about unhealthy Fours, and how this emotional spotlight can look from their viewpoint.

Now, when we are healthy, this is what other Enneagram types say about us:

"I never would have thought you were a Four!"

This is both disappointing and a huge compliment, if they're thinking about unhealthy Fours.

As we've said earlier, other people's reaction to you is beyond your control, especially when they may be reacting out of their own unhealthiness. This is not your fault, but I hope that seeing the reality of a Four's weaknesses will give you a strong desire for growth.

When we look at our own Four-ness objectively, we gain great insight into our own tendencies. We are not all unhealthy, but you should be able to see how you might slide there. Healthy Fours look pretty normal from the outside, which makes it hard to tell them apart from other numbers. This is why most Enneagram teachers teach the negative aspects unique to each type. They're loud and easy to spot.

SHIFT IN FOCUS

We need to choose not to be discouraged by our weaknesses. When you see the descriptions of unhealthy Fours, instead of getting defensive that we are not all like that, use it as a moment to praise God that you're not living in your own worst behaviors. God has helped us to grow and thankfulness can abound.

• • • • • • • • • • • **DAY 34**

What Does God Say About Our Emotions?
By Alison Bradley

> *But you, O LORD, are a shield about me, my glory,*
> *and the lifter of my head. I cried aloud to the LORD,*
> *and he answered me from his holy hill.*
> (Psalm 3:3–4)

When God created man, He said, *"Let us make man in our image, after our likeness"* (Genesis 1:26). As we discussed earlier, this refers to our heart and emotions. *"It was very good,"* God declared (Genesis 1:31). Throughout Scripture, we see evidence of the Lord's emotions. We are told that He is *"gracious and merciful, slow to anger and abounding in steadfast love"* (Psalm 145:8). We especially see His emotions in the person of Jesus. In our current culture, emotions aren't always welcomed. Yet, we can take our cues from Scripture that emotions are not only given by God, but they reflect His nature too.

Emotions are part of our reflection of the Lord and are important messengers about our reality, but they can't be trusted to paint the whole picture of what is going on. Sin has tainted so much that God created as good, and emotions aren't immune from sin's touch. David offers us a model of what it looks like to sort through our emotions throughout the Psalms. And through his prayers, he shows us that the Lord listens to us and responds to our emotions, even if they're part of the consequences for our own sin.

Psalm 3 was written by David as he fled for his life from his own son, so I think it is fair to call this "a psalm of family dysfunction." David certainly played a role, as Absalom's father, in the dire state of their relationship. David's despair, his fear, and his grief are all laid out in Psalm 3. He takes his emotions to the Lord and doesn't hide them, even though he isn't free from fault. But notice what David says in the midst of this dialogue, calling God *a shield about me, my glory, and the lifter of my head.* The Lord not only listens, but He protects and responds to David in his emotional state.

David also shows us what it looks like to turn to the Lord in the depth of emotion, and how the Lord responds to him.

> *I am weary with my moaning; every night I flood my bed with tears; I drench my couch with my weeping. My eye wastes away because of grief; it grows weak because of all my foes. Depart from me, all you workers of evil, for the LORD has heard the sound of my weeping. The LORD has heard my plea; the LORD accepts my prayer.* (Psalm 6:6–9)

David doesn't speak of his circumstances changing at this time, but he speaks of the comfort he received from the Lord.

SHIFT IN FOCUS

Pause and thank the Lord for how He has created you with emotions. Thank Him for how He listens to you and gives you the gift of His presence. Offer up your own prayer or borrow this one, if it reflects your heart:

Dear Heavenly Father, thank You for creating my emotions and that they are good. Help me to reflect Your character with my heart and emotions. Thank You for being a God who listens and doesn't dismiss my emotions or experience, even when I'm at fault. You love me and want to understand me, even when You know my emotions don't tell the whole story. Amen.

DAY 35 • • • • • • • • • • •

Emotions: An Indicator Not a Director
By Alison Bradley

By this we shall know that we are of the truth and reassure our heart
before him; for whenever our heart condemns us, God is greater
than our heart, and he knows everything. Beloved, if our heart does
not condemn us, we have confidence before God.
(1 John 3:19–21)

The day before had been spent crying. It was barely an hour into the morning and tears were seeping out again. It wasn't that it hadn't been talked about or prayed over. It wasn't that I didn't believe truth or wasn't working to trust the Lord. Everything felt out of my control, and I simply felt weary and tired of that being true. As I read my Bible that morning, inviting the Lord in the mess of my emotions and the many things outside of my control, I had an unbidden thought. *I'd rather just stay sad today.*

Have you been there too? As someone who experiences emotions so loudly, it can be hard to not allow them to direct your actions. When there is much that is hard, and when the feelings are loud, it is so tempting to hold tight to your feelings to create some semblance of control. It is tempting to allow your feelings to dictate what you do, but this isn't the role your emotions were created to play.

I love the metaphor of our feelings as messages, coming to tell us something we need to know about ourselves or what is happening in our life. But messages are meant to be the beginning of what happens next, not the beginning and end all rolled up into one. It can be tempting to hold tightly to the emotion, even after it has delivered its message, to keep that spotlight shining inward on how the world is making you feel. You may be tempted to hide in those feelings instead of inviting them to be part of your decisions for your next step. You also need to recognize that your feelings aren't the full picture. They don't tell the entire story of what is real.

SHIFT IN FOCUS

Pause to read 1 John 3:19–21 again. Notice what he says about the heart and truth. Sometimes your heart will speak the same truth that the Lord does about you: you are beloved and have confidence before Him. But sometimes your heart will condemn you, even though the truth remains. Your emotions should not be dismissed, but neither should they dictate your actions without bringing them to the Lord to evaluate what is real. Notice what these verses say about the Lord: He knows everything. He can help you sort out what is true, and what part of your emotions reflect reality.

Consider memorizing these verses to remind your heart that you are beloved and have confidence before the Lord, even if the message from your current emotions says otherwise.

If you are experiencing any loud emotions today, pause and invite the Lord to show you what is true and to release what is not. Invite Him to help you believe what He says about you.

DAY 36 • • • • • • • • • • •

Emotions and Godliness
By Alison Bradley

Why are you cast down, O my soul, and why are you in turmoil
within me? Hope in God; for I shall again praise him,
my salvation and my God.
(Psalm 42:5)

The Psalms offer us permission to experience our emotions. How grateful I am for the way they model what it looks like to be godly and emotional. In Psalm 16:7, David speaks of how his heart and emotions are giving him insight about what to do next. He sees his emotions as a God-given tool of discernment, as he listens to his feelings with the Lord.

Psalm 42 offers a beautiful picture of emotional honesty: *"My tears have been my food day and night, while they say to me all the day long, 'Where is your God?'"* (Psalm 42:3). The psalmist is so honest about his grief, making him question if God even cares for him anymore. Can you relate to that depth of emotion?

The next verse presents a godly response: *"These things remember, as I pour out my soul: how I would go with the throng, and lead them in procession to the house of God and with glad shouts and songs of praise, a multitude keeping festival"* (Psalm 42:4). The psalmist reminds himself of a time in his life when he was not depressed or heartbroken, but easily able to celebrate and rejoice in the Lord. This isn't to diminish his current feelings, but to speak the truth that his emotions don't tell the whole story of who he is or who the Lord is.

The psalmist then preaches to himself: *"Why are you cast down, O my soul, and why are you in turmoil within me? Hope in God; for I shall again praise him, my salvation and my God"* (Psalm 42:5). He offers himself as an example of how to respond to loud emotions. He acknowledges them, but doesn't allow them to have the final say over him. He preaches to his own soul that this will not always be his story.

Be encouraged by this example. Uncooperative or loud emotions do not disqualify you from a godly life. This psalm shows us what it looks like to name our feelings honestly, bringing them to the Lord, even when they don't match what is true.

SHIFT IN FOCUS

What are you feeling today? Take a moment to honestly name what your emotions are telling you.

How can you preach truth to your own heart? Consider one of the following ways to ground yourself in truth today:

+ Meditate on Psalm 86:11–13, which invites the Lord to help you walk in truth, uniting your heart with your intentions to follow Him.

+ Write out a part of your story where you could easily recognize the Lord's love for you.

+ Take a cue from Psalm 42:8, inviting a song to ground you in the truth of God's love.

+ Choose a phrase from Scripture to treat as a breath prayer. If this is new to you, you can begin with Psalm 46:10:

  Inhale. Be still.

  Exhale. Know that I am God.

• • • • • • • • • • • DAY 37

Emotions and Shame

Fear not, for you will not be ashamed; be not confounded, for you will not be disgraced; for you will forget the shame of your youth, and the reproach of your widowhood you will remember no more.
(Isaiah 54:4)

Shame is the core emotion attached to the heart triad, which means that we are plagued by the voice of an *inner-shamer*. We already talked about this a bit on Day 26 ("A Heart Battered by Shame"). Here, I want to explain why this is so heavy for us, and where we can find our hope.

I believe one of the reasons the heart triad is plagued by an inner-shamer is because we are called to show the world a distinct part of the heart of God. This is done through love, helpfulness, giving, encouraging, charming, inspiring, creating, space saving, and being empathetic toward all of God's people. I believe the heart triad is especially designed for this purpose, although this does not mean that those in the head and gut triads have no opportunity to show God's heart to others.

Just like Satan uses envy to sabotage how you reflect God, he uses shame to stop you from showing the world God's heart. God's heart for His people is not only comforting, loving, and beautiful, but His love also draws people to their knees in repentance. (See Romans 2:4.) This means God has won, and Satan has lost. The enemy doesn't like that.

So Satan plagues us with a simple, but very effective tactic. He tells us that we're not good enough, that we'll fail if we try, that we're not worthy of love, and that we might as well not even try. Part of the reason this is so effective is because it's true. Apart from Christ, we are sinful; we can't be enough; we can't win enough, or create enough; we can and will fail. We are made from the dust of the ground; this is a reality.

What we miss when we listen to the lies of shame is this: you are no longer bound by shame; you are no longer mere dust; your sin that you're not enough no longer defines you.

Isaiah 1:18 says, "*Come now, let us reason together, says the* LORD: *though your sins are like scarlet, they shall be as white as snow; though they are red like crimson, they shall become like wool.*"

When Jesus died, He took your dirty clothes and gave you His pure white robe. You don't deserve it. You did nothing to earn it. You are certainly not worthy to wear such a spotless garment, but that no longer matters. Satan's accusations against you about your worth don't take into account that when God looks at you, He sees you as His beloved. What you have done, what you will do, and every way that you are *not enough* no longer matters. Jesus took care of that at the cross; your sins are forgiven.

When you're emotionally derailed by shame and when shame paralyzes you, turn to the gospel to speak truth into the darkness.

"I am enough because God's grace is enough!"

"Even if I fail, I know that the Lord holds me in His hands. Fear will not rule me!"

"God loves me, created me to love, and wants me to be loved."

"I'm significant! The God of the universe created me, loves me, saved me, and calls me His child."

"I will be courageous for the glory of Christ, and whatever He puts my hands to do."

SHIFT IN FOCUS

As painful as it can be, you can engage with your inner-shamer by tracking what it's telling you for a day. All you need is a pen and a piece of paper. This exercise, though simple, is very effective in exposing the lies in what you're hearing. Seeing what your inner-shamer says written out, and not just feeling the impact of the voice in your head, can help you shine the light of truth.

Take a moment and thank God for the gift of His gospel, and ask Him to help you in this fight against your inner-shamer.

Dear Heavenly Father, there are no words to thank You for the gift of being seen as pure in Your sight. I'm in awe of the grace of who I am, and how You've sealed me to be Yours. I'm sorry for the times I believe that my old filthy rags are still "me" and the times I listen to Satan's lies. Lord, I want to live life in light of truth. Help me to fight shame daily, and listen to Your truth instead. Shame does not get the last word, You do! I want to live in the freedom of who You say I am. Amen.

DAY 38 • • • • • • • • • • • •
Emotions and Self-Control

*But the fruit of the Spirit is love, joy, peace, patience, kindness,
goodness, faithfulness, gentleness, self-control;
against such things there is no law.*
(Galatians 5:22–23)

Self-control is commonly known as a fruit of the Spirit. It's the ability to control one's emotions and desires, or the expression of them in one's behavior, especially in difficult situations.

Emotions are hard to control; it takes work, effort, and training. As the mother of a toddler, I can truly speak to this. My son is almost two years old, and he has very strong emotions that he cannot control yet. This leads to every *no* being the end of the world, and things he doesn't understand leading to screaming on the floor. It's exhausting for me, but I also see it being exhausting for him.

The good news is that being a fruit of the Spirit means that self-control is something that the Holy Spirit helps us with. This doesn't mean we have no responsibility to grow in self-control, but it *does* mean we are not alone in our fight to control our reactions. Being in the heart triad means we receive information through our emotions and then, as Fours, we process that emotional hit with more emotion.

If someone tells us, "Oh, I thought you'd be taller," it hits us right in the heart. We feel self-conscious and taken aback; there's a sting of hurt developing. Processing it further with emotions, we might start to feel indignant. We think, *Why would they feel the need to say that? I would never say that.*

We might eventually let this go, but it could take a while, and we might experience the full spectrum of human emotions on the way to being fine.

On the other end of the spectrum, when we watch a great movie for the first time, we may feel awe and wonder that stay with us for days. We may daydream about scenes from the movie and listen to the soundtrack over and over, living on a sort of emotional high.

Now self-control in these two situations looks like:

When someone says, "Oh, I thought you'd be taller," you start to feel self-conscious, but you stop yourself and say, "Oh, that's funny! Nope, this is all of me." Assuming they just said something silly to start the conversation, you let it go. With the Holy Spirit's help, you control the spiral that might've otherwise left you vulnerable and hurting.

Now, in the case of days of daydreaming after a magical movie experience—for me, it would be *The Greatest Showman*— You may be missing out on something, or distracting yourself from something you should be doing by indulging in this fantasy.

Self-control does not mean never indulging, but it is knowing when to stop and say no. Some might call this *adulting* because in the midst of daydreaming, there are groceries to buy, a bank run to make, and a cousin's birthday party to attend. These things you still have to do, in a responsible, timely manner, so keep your daydreaming in check. Set a timer for twenty minutes when you put in headphones to dance around the living room, limit your Pinterest searches to once a day, or limit your soundtrack listening to the car.

SHIFT IN FOCUS

Self-control is something that needs to be practiced. Fruits of the Spirit rarely appear overnight.

Is there an area where you need to be practicing self-control? Negative comments? Daydreaming? Maybe TV or social media?

Are there certain comments that trigger you? Have you ever asked someone why they said what they said and really listened to them?

• • • • • • • • • • • DAY 39

How to Get Out of an Emotional Spiral

Therefore I will not refrain my mouth; I will speak in the anguish of my spirit; I will complain in the bitterness of my soul.
(Job 7:11)

We talked yesterday about self-control and how negative comments can send us into what I like to call an *emotional spiral*.

You're probably familiar with the concept, even if this isn't what you call it. Maybe for you, it's the depths of despair, feeling loudly, or being moody.

I think emotional spiral is a good term because we go spiraling around a certain feeling, event, or circumstance without a way to stop. The longer we circle this problem, the deeper we go into our feelings about it, and a good outlook seems impossible. You may even think, *Will I ever feel okay again?* You might get angry that something so small is affecting you so much.

So how do we stop spiraling?

Step one: Get out of your head and into your body. Go for a run, exercise, take a hot shower—anything that distracts your mind and gets you into your body. This step feels like the worst, but it is essential.

Step two: Pray. If you don't have words, turn on a worship song, and let it lead you into your own words to the Lord. You don't need to be formal, just tell Him what's going on in your heart and ask Him for help.

Step three: Journal or reprocess the events. Just distracting yourself from the problem doesn't make it go away, but it will give you a more objective opinion about what's going on. After you've gotten out of your head and prayed, take another look, think over the series of events, let God give you grace for the other party, and then let it go or take an action toward reconciling the situation.

You'll find that these steps are pretty effective at stopping an emotional spiral. They're *very* hard steps to take in the moment, and they require self-control, but the more you do them, the easier they become.

SHIFT IN FOCUS

The book of Job gives us a great example of an emotional spiral. Was what happened to Job worthy of deep, devastating emotions? Of course. But the more he and his friends spiraled around the problems, and argued over who was to blame, the worse their attitudes became. God eventually had to step in to interrupt Job's pity party with a stern, cold reality check.

If you need a clear reality check today, read God's reply to Job in Job 38–41.

• • • • • • • • • • • DAY 40

How to Live with Godly Purpose and Emotion

For your obedience is known to all, so that I rejoice over you, but I want you to be wise as to what is good and innocent as to what is evil.

(Romans 16:19)

So how do we live in the tension of being Christians who are highly emotional people? There are two different camps on this question.

Camp one says your emotions are super important, and you need to listen to them. It says, "Follow your heart," it will never steer you wrong.

Camp two says your heart is evil, and none of the emotions that come from it are honoring to God. It says, "Don't listen to your heart; it'll only lead you to evil."

These camps are the two sides of the pendulum, and we need to live in the middle.

We need to listen to our emotions because they are a great indicator of other things going on inside us, but we don't take our emotions as 100 percent truth, and we don't listen to them or act on them when they oppose what God says in His Word.

Something to keep in mind with this question of godliness and emotions is that God made you exactly the way you are, and He has a purpose for your empathy, emotions, and expressive spirit. (See Jeremiah 29:11.) I want to encourage you again, this is a *good* thing, and your emotions reflect God.

However, we can't let our emotions become our master. (See Matthew 6:24.) That job is already taken: we have an almighty

God and should listen to Him above all else. Our emotions are fickle, frustrating, and ever-changing. Listen to them, hear them out, then dismiss them or act on them with God's guidance.

We don't worship our emotions and express them without any sort of a filter.

We don't demonize emotions and repress them so we even convince ourselves we aren't feeling them.

It doesn't matter how you feel, if God says no, then we obey, not out of blind duty but because our God loves us. He has the best plans for us, and if He says no, then we fight to believe that is what's best for us.

SHIFT IN FOCUS

Some Christians go too far and treat emotions as a wild animal to be caged and never let out.

However, Jesus laughed, He cried, He yelled, He loved, and He preached with passion; unlike us, He did it all without sinning. There is not one time that Jesus gave into sin, which also tells us that emotions are not the issue, but what we do with them can be a problem.

Have you been hurt by Christians who believe emotions should be caged? Or have you watched other Christians who do not believe that their emotions need to be under the submission of Christ, who follow their feelings into devastation and sin?

Although we may sin in our emotions and reactions, with God's help, we can hold the good and let go of the bad. May He grant us a healthy emotional life, in His name. Amen!

10 Days of Saying No to Manipulation

Going to Two in Stress

• • • • • • • • • • • **DAY 41**

Seasons of Growth

There is a time for everything, and a season for every activity under the heavens: a time to be born and a time to die, a time to plant and a time to uproot, a time to kill and a time to heal, a time to break down and a time to build, a time to weep and a time to laugh, a time to mourn and a time to dance, a time to scatter stones and a time to gather them, a time to embrace and a time to refrain from embracing, a time to search and a time to give up, a time to keep and a time to throw away, a time to tear and a time to mend, a time to be silent and a time to speak, a time to love and a time to hate, a time for war and a time for peace.

(Ecclesiastes 3:1–8 NIV)

In the whirlwind of life, expectations, and demands, it can be hard to think of ourselves as living seasonally. We live on an earth with winter, spring, summer and fall, and we observe and celebrate the earth and its seasons, but we rarely give ourselves the same permission to change and transform. Instead, we expect all or nothing. Either I am … or I am not. There is right now, and anything worth doing is worth doing today. This is especially the mentality in the hustle of America.

Of course, as we look back on our life, seasons are evident. There was that really hard year of illness, there were years of singleness, there was that amazing three months of falling in love, there were years with little kids, there were years of learning … everything in its own season.

We have a lot to learn from the way God created the earth with its seasons. In Ecclesiastes 3:1–8, we read that there is a season for everything, and we know God is talking about us, not just the earth. For every bad and hard season, there is a season of rest and good to come.

SHIFT IN FOCUS

In the next nine days, we will go into detail about what seasons of stress look like for you as a Four.

As you look at your own life today, what season are you in? Read the verses from Ecclesiastes again and pick one or two adjectives that represent the season you're in.

Are you mourning or celebrating? Transitioning or resting? Uprooting or planting?

If you're in a more hopeful, joyful, and restful season, it may be time to press into growth and celebrate the growth you can see in yourself. If you're in a season of hard transition and survival, it will be helpful for you to see this time as a passing season and discover hope on the horizon. You may see some ways that you're growing even in stress and adversity. Celebrate those wins!

• • • • • • • • • • • • **DAY 42**

What Is a Season of Stress?

So he bowed their hearts down with hard labor; they fell down, with
none to help. Then they cried to the LORD in their trouble, and he
delivered them from their distress. He brought them out of darkness
and the shadow of death, and burst their bonds apart.
(Psalm 107:12–14)

In talking about the seasons of life, we all know that there are seasons of great stress.

When we talk about stress using Enneagram verbiage, we aren't talking about being late for work or losing your keys. We all get frustrated and irritable in those circumstances. No, when the Enneagram refers to stress, it means seasonal stress, such as losing your job, transitioning, losing a loved one, and so forth. In those times, we're in survival mode, often for months or years.

During seasons of stress, dear Four, you may feel that suddenly all of your relationships are black and white. You start noticing all the ways people don't return your affection and it stings; you can't stop thinking about it. You feel clingy; you have extravagant gift ideas and overspend on gifts; you feel the urge to fulfill everyone's needs in order to receive thanks, praise, or admiration.

These behaviors should work as a stoplight for you to ask yourself a couple of questions:

+ What is stressing me out right now?

+ Am I in a season of stress?

+ If I could look back on *me in stress*, how would I be kinder to the people in my life?

+ Where should I be resting or giving myself more grace in this season?

We should not be ashamed of seasons of stress. If anything, they move us to cling to God in a precious way and become more aware of our need for Him.

SHIFT IN FOCUS

Take a couple of moments to reflect on the season you're in right now. Is this a season of growth for you or a season of stress?

If it's a season of stress take a deep breath, be kind to your battered heart, and cling to your Savior.

• • • • • • • • • • • • DAY 43

How Do I Go to Two in Stress?

But when you give to the needy,
do not let your left hand know what your right hand is doing.
(Matthew 6:3)

How does it look to *go to Two* in stress? For Fours, going to Two can manifest in relationships, but not in a good way. Suddenly, all of your relationships appear to be black and white; they love you or they hate you. You're hurt that someone you haven't thought of in months hasn't reached out to you. Or your spouse didn't meet your ideal birthday plans, and it's the end of the world. You wonder if they even love you anymore.

Another side effect is that you might be more attuned to the practical needs of others than before. While this should be a good thing, your stressed-out self might use these opportunities to help fill up your love tank with praise and admiration. You might bait someone for an affirmation, or hint that you would appreciate a grand gesture of affection. You may just want this person to like you more so they'll be there for you. Not trusting that you, by yourself, are enough to get them to stay.

When others don't respond in the way you hoped or seem more distant than normal, it can cause astronomical hurt; the repercussions can actually end up ruining relationships.

It's important to recognize these stress behaviors because we might not realize we are in a stressful season until it's over. When you are aware of stress, you can give yourself a little grace. You're not in a season of growth right now, so stop beating yourself up!

When you catch yourself acting out in Two, you can change the pattern of your response, or at least be aware that your emotional reactions at this time are not logically sound. Remember, when you're stressed, things bother you that wouldn't if you had more grace and room in your life to process. Catching yourself reacting in stress, instead of choosing to respond in an unhealthy way, can save you and others a world of hurt.

SHIFT IN FOCUS

Reflect on a past season of stress. How did these behaviors hinder you during that time?

How might recognizing these behaviors as a stress indicator change your actions in the future?

If you are experiencing a season of stress currently, pray to the Lord to guide you through it.

DAY 44

The Struggles of Type Two
By Christine Rollings

For am I now seeking the approval of man, or of God? Or am I
trying to please man? If I were still trying to please man, I would
not be a servant of Christ.
(Galatians 1:10)

Twos are often portrayed as the most loving, selfless, and most generous types of the Enneagram. Always being there with a helping hand, they are aware of the needs of those around them. Their boldness in loving others, superpower of foreseeing needs before they even appear, and generally kind disposition makes them the friend everyone wants to have.

But Twos aren't always the easiest to have around. Their ache for love and affection often results in manipulation to get it. Their ability to be in tune with the needs around them leaves them feeling lonely and unloved when that care isn't returned, even if the need for a return wasn't explicitly implied.

As a Two, on a good day, I am very aware of the needs of those around me and eager to meet those needs. This is a way that I reflect the heart of God. But on a day when I am struggling, I expect others to see *my* needs and meet them without me asking. If I don't get the help that I expect, I will use manipulation to try and get what I want, although I may not realize it until later! I feel angry and uncared for when others don't see my needs; it makes me feel invisible, while the other person is left in the dark about why I am upset.

I struggle with depending on the approval of others, wanting to please them more than I want to please God. I want to feel love and affirmation from those in my life in order to feel whole, which gives the people in my life far too much power.

While an Enneagram Two goes to a Four as they grow in their creativity, a Four goes to a Two in seasons of stress, attempting to fill their emptiness with the love and approval of others. This is why, dear Four, as you read these struggles of a type Two, you may be able to relate to them during your seasons of stress.

SHIFT IN FOCUS

Do you have any type Twos in your life?

What are their best qualities?

How do you relate to this longing for others to make you feel whole?

• • • • • • • • • • • • DAY 45
The Temptation of Manipulation

Go to the flock and bring me two good young goats, so that I may
prepare from them delicious food for your father,
such as he loves. And you shall bring it to your father to eat,
so that he may bless you before he dies.
(Genesis 27:9–10)

Manipulation means to influence events, thoughts, or behaviors without making your motives or intentions clear. It's a form of masterful trickery, and to those who use it, it feels altogether necessary.

When thinking of manipulation, I often think of the story of Rebekah and Jacob in Genesis 27, in which they tricked Isaac into blessing Jacob instead of Esau. This was a manipulative and cunning move on their part, and the validity of their actions is of great theological dispute. However, I think we can all agree that Isaac was very hurt and angered by their actions.

Today, manipulation might not look like a battle for a blessing. But it's manipulation when you text someone to tell them you're thinking of them, and then get mad when they don't return the text in kind. You wanted them to think of you, you wanted the affirmation of a well-worded text, and you hid these desires behind a compliment, giving them something they had no way of knowing they needed to repay.

It's also manipulation when you buy a huge birthday present for someone, and daydream about how excited they'll be and how positively they'll think of you once they receive it. You're trying to influence their future behaviors with your current ones, but you're not being honest about it. You might as well sign the card, "You owe me!"

Manipulation, over time, turns into a dangerous habit. You may not realize that your little manipulative tendencies have turned into a monster, destroying relationships, and everything you were trying to build by using it.

It's pretty easy to spot manipulation when it's happening to you, but it can be hard to spot it in the moment when you're the one doing the manipulating. This is why we need to let things go because we often don't realize there were strings attached until we don't get what we wanted. Expectations can be the true thief of joy when it comes to giving.

Letting go looks like audibly telling yourself that you won't be upset if your text isn't returned as you send it. Letting go looks like being humble in your generosity, not expecting anything in return. Letting go looks like telling the truth about your intentions and what you need.

Sending the following text would be much more honest than trying to bait the recipient with a compliment: "I'm having a really rough day, and I'm struggling to remember what God says about my worth. Could you pray for me?"

If they don't reply, that's okay. We don't like to be this vulnerable because we are afraid of the hurt of no response, but we can cling to our Savior even if that is the case. Your friend might very well be praying for you, but they didn't get a chance to text back. We all have those days, and assuming the best is good medicine for any healthy relationship.

SHIFT IN FOCUS

Pray and ask God to expose manipulative tendencies in your heart.

Dear Heavenly Father, I pray that You will expose my tendency to manipulate others in stress. Please expose these things even as they're happening. I want to be generous like You, I want to be honest, and I don't want to use people. Please convict me of this, and lead me to You in my stress and insecurities. Amen.

DAY 46 • • • • • • • • • • • •

The Temptation of Black and White Relational Thinking

Whoever walks in integrity will be delivered,
but he who is crooked in his ways will suddenly fall.
(Proverbs 28:18)

As Fours in stress, we often struggle with black and white relational thinking. There are those who love you ... and everyone else must not.

For my sixteenth birthday, I was only going to invite people who I felt had *loved me well* during the year leading up to it. Mom quickly stopped this plan, but it revealed some very strong black and white relational thinking. I wanted a visualization of all the people who met my expectations of love, and I wanted everyone else to feel bad and try harder to love me more. Of course, I had never told any of these people they were under a performance review or my expectations of our relationship, but I held them to that standard anyway. This black and white relational thinking is something we do in stress, and it can be very damaging.

This type of thinking says:

+ "You better meet my expectations without me having to communicate them."

+ "You better meet my expectations without me having to initiate anything."

+ "You better pour into me constantly, or I will be hurt."

+ "I will not have grace for the seasons of *your* life."

+ "You must want a relationship with me no matter what."

+ "I will not waste my time pouring into you unless I'm reciprocating what you're already doing."

These times of great stress seem to draw a line in our thinking. Either I have no grace for you, or I have abundant grace for you. There is no in between.

These seasons also uncover a lot of selfishness in how we may be approaching relationships. It's easy for us to stop trying and see what happens. Either the relationship will dissolve, and we'll take that as proof that what our shame says is correct, or the other party will step up, and we'll feel like we're on cloud nine. This is using people in the worst way.

You may have heard of the push-pull tendencies that Fours have, and this is part of it. We will pull people close, then let go and see what happens. This is an unhealthy behavior of Fours, but we also see a glimpse of it in stress.

What we need is abundant grace, both for ourselves and others. Your friend might be going through a rough season and hasn't had time to catch lunch or even reach out recently. This doesn't impact how much she cares about you. If you can step back and try to think of their side, you can have more grace without assuming motivations.

We also need to have grace for ourselves in this season. You're surviving. Your brain is trying to cling to things that are safe and prune the rest. There is nothing wrong with you; you're just surviving. But thinking graciously about others will help! They may not need to be pruned just yet.

SHIFT IN FOCUS

Are there people you've unfairly pushed out of your life in a season of stress?

Reflect on how you might apologize to them.

• • • • • • • • • • • • DAY 47

The Temptation of Unrealistic Expectations

If we say we have no sin, we deceive ourselves,
and the truth is not in us.
(1 John 1:8)

The problem with being a romantic idealist is that sometimes we are living so deeply in our daydream that we don't realize we've idealized it until it's not happening like we had dreamed it would.

Whether it's a wedding, holiday, job interview, or a casual Saturday night at home, it's hard to find a Four who doesn't have a *feel* for what ideal would be, even if they may not be able to explain it. Dear Fours, we are confusing, and we know it! When we are stressed and our thinking turns very relational, it's no longer about events and décor, but about how people treat us, or how they show us love to meet our expectations.

Maybe it's as simple as, "If my husband loved me, he'd let me sleep in tomorrow." Or maybe it's as complicated as, "If my mom loved me, she'd stop drinking."

Either way, these expectations, especially when they're not communicated, are very likely not going to be met.

Those we love can't read our minds, and if we're having a hard time expressing what we want, then it's impossible for them to have a gauge on what would make us happy. Expectations without communication is just a setup for disappointment.

One anniversary, I had a thought, "I wonder if my husband will bring flowers home for me?"

At that moment, I stopped myself and asked, "Do I want flowers?" The answer was "Yes!"

I knew, for the health of my marriage, that I had to make a choice. Either I was going to tell my husband I wanted flowers, or I was going to let him surprise me … maybe with flowers. I decided to let him surprise me. I was pretty sure he had flowers on his mind, but no. No flowers.

I was so thankful that I promised myself not to be upset. I hugged him, and never said anything about wanting flowers; I just bought some for myself the next week. Next time, I will ask; I will verbalize my desires so my husband has the tools to love me well. I know he would always bring me flowers if I asked him, and he can't read my mind.

It may be more romantic to be surprised, or it might feel more fulfilling not to have to communicate, but waiting with expectations will cause you a world of hurt.

SHIFT IN FOCUS

What's the next holiday? What's something you wished someone had done for you on this holiday last year? Could you ask for that thing?

The more you practice asking for what you want, the easier it will be to ask, and those who love you will start to learn more about what you really want.

• • • • • • • • • • • DAY 48

When You're Tempted to Discount Your Need for Love
By Christine Rollings

Are not five sparrows sold for two pennies? And not one of them is forgotten before God. Why, even the hairs of your head are all numbered. Fear not; you are of more value than many sparrows.
(Luke 12:6–7)

Dear Four, in a season of stress, you may be tempted to discount your need for love. It may be easier to focus on the needs of those around you, neglecting your own for fear of not being seen or those needs not being met. You might tell yourself that you are not worthy of being loved, or you may busy yourself with loving others so you don't even think about it.

Here's the thing: you have every right to embrace and name your need for love. This is a natural human desire and longing. This need feels vulnerable, since it isn't up to us to meet it at all! It may feel counterintuitive to ask for this need to be met, but you really desire others to know how to do it and want to do it.

But often, others not showing you love in the way you desire it doesn't mean that they don't love you. They just may not know how to show it, and you have every right to ask. Do you need to ask your wife for an evening out alone with friends? Do you need to ask your husband for a bouquet? Do you want a coffee date with an old acquaintance? If those things make you feel loved, don't discount those desires! Ask for them!

We love because God first loved us. (See 1 John 4:19.) We begin our relationships with a foundation of being loved. We need that love from God! He designed us that way to draw us into relationship with Himself. We can rest in that need that is already met in Him as we approach our need in relationships.

SHIFT IN FOCUS

Do you find yourself discounting your need for love in seasons of stress? Do you notice it when it happens, or do you busy yourself with helping other people, showing your love and hoping it will be reciprocated?

What will make you feel loved the next time this happens? Make a plan to ask your loved one for what you need.

• • • • • • • • • • DAY 49

Acknowledging the Problem

*The saying is trustworthy and deserving of full acceptance,
that Christ Jesus came into the world to save sinners,
of whom I am the foremost.*
(1 Timothy 1:15)

As we mentioned earlier, acknowledging our need for change is the first step toward changing. It's impossible to change if we remain unaware, or insist on behaving in ways that hurt ourselves or others.

I know this has been true for me and my Enneagram journey. When my negative stress behaviors were first laid out before me, I wanted to hide and make excuses for my tendencies. However, as I watched my own life, I couldn't help but see the truth. My heart would distract itself from stress by focusing on others and my perception of their lack of love for me. I would fixate and manipulate to get the love my heart longed for, all the while not acknowledging that it was love I desperately craved.

I wasn't noticing lack of affection toward me because it was new or worse than before. I wasn't keeping others accountable. I wasn't upholding high standards. I wasn't righting wrongs. I was just going about getting love in all the wrong ways. Wanting to be loved is not a bad desire, but we can go about it in a way that is not only unhelpful but sinful. I was unknowingly causing myself and others a lot of pain. Now, even though I've acknowledged the problem, sometimes I still choose the route of pain because it's familiar and often feels safer than asking for what I need. However, seeing this problem and being able to name it as it's happening has helped me to make much healthier choices.

I can backtrack to try to figure out where my stress is coming from. I ask myself, "Is there some action I need to take here?" I go to God in prayer about it and trust Him to fill my heart with the love it needs. I consider these choices:

+ I can choose to ask for a hug instead of buying a gift just hoping that the recipient will give me a proverbial pat-on-the-back.

+ I can ask questions and have a conversation instead of jumping to assumptions, even if my heart feels ready to burn that bridge.

+ I can give myself grace, and treat my heart gently as it's fragile and in need of care.

SHIFT IN FOCUS

Have you ever verbally affirmed your need for love? Whether the answer is yes or no, repeat this phrase out loud now, and the next time you find yourself using negative stress behaviors:

"There is nothing wrong with needing love. God made us to be in loving relationships with Himself and others. I can ask for this love from others, and also trust that I am already receiving it from God."

• • • • • • • • • • • DAY 50

Surviving Without Burning Bridges

So whatever you wish that others would do to you, do also to them,
for this is the Law and the Prophets.
(Matthew 7:12)

Dear Four, have you ever burned a bridge in a season of stress that you now regret? As you've been reading about these behaviors during the last nine days, maybe someone has come to mind. I'm not talking about cutting off a relationship with an abusive person. If that ended for you during a season of stress, then that's a grace that God gave you during that season. I'm talking about petty or trivial disagreements between friends, or slights that got blown out of proportion, and now you no longer have that friendship.

Maybe you've been hurt by a situation like this, and maybe you've caused it. As you think of those relationships, how do they make you feel? Are you struggling with guilt over this relationship? Do you still feel the anger and resentment? Are you at peace? Maybe you swing through all three of these feelings in a weekend. Whatever you feel, and no matter how close the pain that this person caused, there is probably a sliver of regret over how you handled setting that bridge ablaze. Passion, anger, and hurt don't tend to lead to the most humble and kind endings. Maybe you know this too well. You may not be able to fix the past, but you can move forward with awareness that this is a tendency of yours.

Every situation that comes up and brings this familiar sting of hurt will be different, but keep the verse above close to your heart.

You would want to be given the benefit of the doubt.

You would want to know if you did something that hurt someone else.

You would want your friends to assume the best about you.

You would want others to be able to see all of you and not just a mistake.

You would want to be forgiven.

As you go forward, understanding the nature of loving others means there will be hurt. Try to give your friends and family what you would want them to give you.

Ask for love, give them the tools to love you well, and assume the best.

Stress is not your master, and it doesn't get to ruin your relationships.

SHIFT IN FOCUS

Whose names keep coming to mind as you read about your negative stress behaviors? Write your strongest emotion regarding them beside their names.

_____

_____

_____

Pray for them by name and ask Jesus to help you apologize for your part in the hurt, or to give you peace about the relationship. Their name is on your heart for a reason. Maybe there is reconciliation that could happen in that relationship, or maybe God wants you to let go of the hurt and move forward. Either way, learn from these situations and consider how you could have changed the outcome if you had assumed the best.

10 Days of Growing in Discipline
Going to One in Growth

Seasons of Growth

> *Every good gift and every perfect gift is from above,
> coming down from the Father of lights, with whom
> there is no variation or shadow due to change.*
> (James 1:17)

Thinking of your life in seasonal terms is not only biblical, but it also gives you a lot more grace and hope for your circumstances. Seasons of stress are the opposite of seasons of growth. The latter are periods in your life in which you feel as if you have room to breathe, have more energy, and can focus on spiritual, mental, and physical growth.

Seasons of growth are often blurry or over-romanticized when we look back at our life as a whole. We either can't remember a time in our life that we didn't feel the hum of anxiety and stress, or we can't live fully in the present because no season will ever be as good as it has been in the past.

Both of these thought processes are unfruitful because they're extremes. There is always a mixture of good and bad in every situation; only the details change. This is a result of living in a fallen world. We are living outside of our natural habitat, and it often feels like a paradox of good and bad at the same time.

Now, this doesn't mean that seasons of stress and growth coexist all the time; often, they don't. Circumstances in our lives often tip the scales. Nothing is ever all bad or all good. Working in a toxic environment or the death of a loved one will send us into a season of stress. Likewise, getting our dream job, hitting a sweet spot with parenting, or flourishing in a good friendship can tip the scale to seasons of growth.

During seasons of growth, we should push ourselves. Have you wanted to read a certain book or join a Bible study? Do it! Have you been waiting to start a diet or go to the gym? Now is the time! We literally have more mental space, more energy, and more bandwidth when we are in seasons of growth.

In seasons of growth, we can also see and build a lot of encouraging behaviors. Press into these behaviors and nurture them so that they'll stick beyond this season. Create good habits that will help in future stressful times. Consistent Bible reading is a must for all of life, but especially in those stressed-out days when we feel lost.

Growth seasons are the days of digging deep and reaping rewards. These seasons are gifts from a heavenly Father who loves us and wants to give us good things. We should be using these seasons of good gifts to not only build up our faith but also to help others. (See 1 Peter 4:10.) In the next nine days, we'll see how going to the number One in growth helps Fours to build up themselves and others.

———————————————

SHIFT IN FOCUS

Are you currently in a season of growth?

Do you have a couple of good seasons in your past that you may be over-romanticizing, or may be ungrateful for?

DAY 52 ● ● ● ● ● ● ● ● ● ● ●

How Fours Go to One in Growth

For the moment all discipline seems painful rather than pleasant,
but later it yields the peaceful fruit of righteousness to those who
have been trained by it.
(Hebrews 12:11)

Do you know many Ones? Whether your interactions with Ones have been good or bad will probably dictate how excited you are for these coming devotions.

Ones, especially those who are unhealthy, are thought to be no fun. They have a lot of rules, are pretty serious, and have very high standards that can lead them to *preaching* at others. All of these stereotypes might make you cringe at the thought of becoming more like a One, but trust me, a little One-ness can do great things for you, like lighting the fuse on your firework. You can't truly shine without the positive behaviors of a One. This is how God wired you.

So what does going to One look like?

+ It looks like discipline, consistency, and drive becoming easier for you as you grow.

+ It looks like feeling secure and peaceful in a clean/organized beautiful space.

+ It means the voice of Ones will be very helpful to help you herd the chaos in your mind at times.

+ It looks like not losing your Four-ness, but your Four-ness becoming more purposeful and action-oriented.

+ It means organizing or cleaning *can* give you energy. This is why when you start, it can sometimes be hard to stop.

+ It means not caring what others think, but knowing what's right, and what's yours to do.

+ It looks like confidence.

+ It looks like caring enough about justice to do something.

One-ness equals action. For Fours, who are often paralyzed by shame or envy, action is a necessity for our spiritual growth.

SHIFT IN FOCUS

Our soul naturally points us to this path of growth; it's as if deep down, we know we need the healthy parts of One to help us feel secure and purposeful. You probably already have some One-ish habits.

Which of Ones' behaviors that we mentioned do you recognize in your day-to-day life?

DAY 53 • • • • • • • • • • •

The Best of Type One

This God—his way is perfect; the word of the LORD proves true; he is a shield for all those who take refuge in him.
(2 Samuel 22:31)

Healthy Ones are a delight. They're problem solvers, and they fix things the rest of us didn't even know were broken. They have an eye for organization and process improvement. They notice things, they take action, and they have a great sense of humor. (After all, they go to Enneagram Seven, the Enthusiast, in growth.)

Enneagram Ones are called the Perfectionist, but most don't relate to this title. Yes, they want rules to be followed and everything to make sense, but every type One has different rules and processes that are important to them. Not all Ones are super tidy, or on time. It all depends on their individual rules, and how those play out for them. While some Ones will be very conscientious about grammar, for example, others may be more concerned about driving courtesy.

Why are we talking so much about Ones? Well, since you go to One in growth, learning about them is learning more about yourself. When you're growing, you have access to all of the good attributes of this number, and the more you learn about them, the more you'll be able to spot these traits in yourself.

I am married to an Enneagram One, and I can tell you that he is so helpful to me. Yes, there is some clashing when both of our unhealthy traits meet, or when we assume the other will think the same way we do, but for the most part, we are in a beautiful dance of strengths and weaknesses that balance each other out.

Dear Four, we need the best parts of One. If you have a One who is close to you, they're likely to be the person you need when you're emotionally spiraling. Ones have a gentle logic that is both understanding and helpful. Isn't it cool that God made different types of people, and our strengths can show up and help in others' weaknesses?

SHIFT IN FOCUS

Which of One's strengths do you feel would be most helpful to you?

Do you have a One (or Ones) in your life whom you can go to in crisis? What about people you follow on social media?

DAY 54 • • • • • • • • • • •

Growing in Discipline

An overseer, as God's steward, must be above reproach.
He must not be arrogant ... but hospitable, a lover of good,
self-controlled, upright, holy, and disciplined.
(Titus 1:7–8)

Have you ever been discouraged by your lack of discipline in a certain area? Some areas are more obvious than others, such as your eating habits, your finances, or your time spent on social media. But what I've heard echoed by many Fours is a longing for discipline in Bible reading, prayer, church attendance, or checking in on people they love.

They wonder, "How do I not let *not feeling like it* derail me?"

Why do Fours struggle with some discipline? In part, it's due to our creative nature. Our brains simply don't like to do the same thing twice, which isn't very conducive to forming good habits. However, the other problem we face is that, along with Fives and Nines, we are considered *action repressed*. This means that *thinking* and *feeling* seem like actions, and we often skip the step of taking the action. It also means that the mundane is hard for us. Things that need to be done daily—cleaning the dishes, making the bed, reading the Bible—feel purposeless to some degree, and we struggle with motivation to do them.

Discipline is not only something that we have access to as we go to One, but being a more disciplined Four leads to a lot of personal growth in many areas.

I often have my Four clients ask, "So are schedules, planners, and organized habits helpful to me?" Dear Four, if you're asking this question, you already know the answer—*yes*! However, you must find a system that works for you, something you're excited about that feeds your creativity and has some aspect of accountability.

I don't have a specific day planner or program that will solve action repression, but I do want to encourage you to do *something*. Don't just assume you'll eventually pick up discipline on your own. You have to take steps, act, and do the work.

In Titus 1:8, we read a list of qualifications for elders in the church, but don't let that stop you from longing, praying, and working toward these same qualities. These are things God cares about, and they are good things that are for our benefit and God's glory when they are present in our lives. Whatever discipline needs to look like for you, it will likely be painful in the beginning, but the rewards are more than worth the growing pains.

SHIFT IN FOCUS

What scares you the most about the word *discipline*?

What's one area of your life where you long for discipline?

Have you prayed about this?

Do you have an action plan or accountability to help you?

DAY 55 • • • • • • • • • • • •

Growing in Integrity

Whoever walks in integrity walks securely,
but he who makes his ways crooked will be found out.
(Proverbs 10:9)

I have to confess that authenticity and integrity don't always go hand in hand for me. As a child, I loved to make up stories, and I always got a thrill out of other kids believing my far-fetched tales.

I didn't get into much trouble because I was smart enough to pick my targets so that I didn't get caught—kids like a random girl playing in the McDonald's Playplace, a cute boy in Sunday school whose parents didn't know mine, or my aunt's boyfriend's son who came to one Thanksgiving dinner but probably wouldn't be coming to another. You get my point!

Call it a mix of a creative mind, quick tongue, boredom, and the need to be special, but I was really good at making others believe my stories. These fibs would later morph into prank phone calls in my teenage years, and eventually little lies to protect myself from conflict, especially at work. I'm not proud of any of this, but I'm baring this part of myself with the hope that you might recognize part of your own story in mine.

Integrity is something God has been working on in my heart, and as I grow towards One, I know that's helping me in this area. Ones will do the right thing, even if it makes them look stupid or isn't the popular choice. I want to be like this. I don't want to need others' affirmation so much that I'm willing to lie to get it.

I don't want to care about being seen as special more than I care about being honest. I don't want to excuse sin because it doesn't always *feel* like sin. I don't want to lie just because I'm good at it and it's convenient.

First and foremost, I want my life to glorify God, and that means that I need to choose integrity and truth every time.

Dear Four, do you struggle with integrity? With telling the truth? With people pleasing? Maybe you don't, and that's great! You may be further along in your growth than I am in this area. But if you struggle like me, then I want you to know that integrity in within your reach, that your desire for integrity is godly, and that you don't need to cover yourself in the makeup of lies to matter.

When others discover our lie, it only confirms what we fear about ourselves, and what shame is already telling us. Lying is something that separates us from God, and it's big enough—yes, even the little lies—that Jesus had to die because of it.

Growing in integrity looks like making a choice to tell the truth even when it's uncomfortable, and it's shifting how important you view truthfulness. No, your friend, your boss, or the girl at McDonald's may never know that you lied, but God does. Every day we need to decide that He matters more than the thrill of impressing someone, lying because we are bored, or getting out of something.

———————————————

SHIFT IN FOCUS

Do you struggle with integrity?

Do you have a lapse in integrity that constantly hangs over your head?

If this is a struggle in your life, spend a moment in prayer over this moment of self-awareness, lest Satan uses it to further shame you.

Dear Heavenly Father, I thank You that I have become aware of this sinful part of my heart. It's painful to look at, and it's horribly ugly, but I know that You have forgiven me and can change me by the power of Your Holy Spirit. Please help my heart to value integrity and truth above all else. I long to glorify and honor You in all that I do. Please help this to be an area of supernatural growth in my life. Amen.

• • • • • • • • • • • **DAY 56**

Growing in Consistency

Jesus Christ is the same yesterday and today and forever.
(Hebrews 13:8)

Dear Four, are you a consistent person? I think I would have answered yes before I got married. I felt pretty consistent, the way I did things made sense to me, and I did them regularly enough.

It wasn't until I saw my husband in daily action that I realized how haphazardly I tend to do things. For instance, I don't really have a rhyme or reason for how I make the bed or when it happens. I do it when I feel like it, and how I feel like doing it. This was something I have explained to my husband many times, and he still doesn't understand.

Do you do things when you feel like it? There is nothing consistent about how our feelings ebb and flow around things like the small disciplines of household chores, working out, or other mundane tasks, other than maybe the constant hum of "I'd rather not."

Consistency means something is done in the same way, unchanging over time, with no contradictions. I could start sweating as I read that because nothing in that description sounds like me. I may be somewhat consistent in how I react emotionally to life, what I desire, or how I care about the aesthetics of my world. At least my husband would call these things about me predictable.

However, when it comes to loading the dishwasher, what day I do laundry, budgeting, how I rest, or even how I get into the car, my creative mind subconsciously says, "Let's try something new this time," or "Eww, just like last time—boring!" I don't try to be inconsistent, but any regular pattern of behavior feels like *work*.

This is where type One comes in. My husband puts on his jacket with the exact same motion every day, he always puts his towel in the same place, and he insists that dishes go into the dishwasher a certain way. Inconsistency is against his very nature, and while sometimes I look at him in horror, like he's chained to some awful monster that's draining his soul, I know I need a bit of this consistency too.

Ones reflect God by being consistent. Hebrews 13:8 tells us, *"Jesus Christ is the same yesterday and today and forever."* We benefit greatly from our unchanging, consistent God, and the world benefits greatly from those who don't need to *feel like it* in order to act.

How unstoppable would I be if the little habits in life weren't such a big deal? If I just did them without thinking? I would be a much more impactful and effective person if I spent less time procrastinating or *feeling* about the mundane parts of life and simply developed consistent habits. This is what growing to One gives us. With time, the monotony of repetition can feel purposeful, right, and even comforting.

I find that instead of digging deep and doing the work, consistency is something that just becomes more attractive as we Fours grow to One. It's when we start noticing how our inconsistencies hinder us, and decide to put systems in place to provide a mode of operation throughout the day, that we will feel less hindered or overwhelmed by everything there is to do in our lives.

SHIFT IN FOCUS

Would you call yourself a consistent person?

Why or why not?

What's one area of your life where *not feeling like it* can be a major hindrance to you?

DAY 57 • • • • • • • • • • • •

Growing in Action

Therefore, preparing your minds for action,
and being sober-minded, set your hope fully on the grace
that will be brought to you at the revelation of Jesus Christ.
(1 Peter 1:13)

Dear Four, what does action mean to you?

As we've noted, Fours struggle with emotion, and the process of thinking that *feeling* is action. The crucial last step of actually taking action can be overlooked when we are exhausted, or perhaps satisfied with how we are feeling. Taking that step of action can also be scary, hard, or just not necessary after a satisfying vent session with a close friend. Sometimes this is a conflict when you are with family, applying for jobs, making a big decision, or doing a chore. No matter what the situation, you may be aware of your adverse reaction toward action.

How many projects have you delayed with procrastination? How many relationships are you unhappy with but have never talked to them about the problem? How many areas of your life do you wish were different? Probably more than you'd care to count.

What ends up being a huge detriment to us is that when we stay in the thinking and feeling steps of solving a problem, we stay *in* the problem. These problems don't get solved until we are backed into a corner and explode, often with way more emotion than the situation warrants.

When you go through the correct steps of taking action, then you can respond instead of react:

1. Feel

2. Think

3. Pray

4. Act

Going to One means growing in action. Literally, every aspect of growing to One looks like some sort of action. As we've already discussed, you can't gain discipline or consistency without some sort of action on your part. God was so wise to make a Four's path to growth have very little to do with feeling our way through life, which is something we are already quite good at. No, what we need is action. Growing in action is so important for us because it makes us more effective. Action gets us out of our heads, instead of focusing so much on how things make us feel. When we choose to act, it can be hard, and we might wonder if it's worth it. This is what Satan wants you to believe. However, growth is waiting for you on the other side of obedient action.

SHIFT IN FOCUS

Personally, some of the most defining, growing moments in my life have revolved around some action that I took. There is one situation in my life where everything in me wanted to stay in the spiral of feeling and thinking, and never taking action. It was finally a moment of trusting in God that led me to action, even with shaking hands and quivering lips. This situation was and still is very hard; nevertheless, I have never regretted taking action.

Maybe you have a story like this too?

Is there somewhere in your life that you need to move on from feeling and thinking to praying and acting?

• • • • • • • • • • • • **DAY 58**

Finding Your Organized and Beautiful Space

In the fourth year the foundation of the house of the LORD was laid …. And in the eleventh year… the house was finished in all its parts, and according to all its specifications.
(1 Kings 6:37–8)

Have you ever noticed that you feel lighter, clearer, maybe even more peaceful in organized and beautiful spaces?

Whether you're thinking of a museum with beautiful paintings, an aesthetically pleasing coffee shop, or your own house right after you've done a thorough cleaning, you likely know nothing can beat the feeling that cleanliness and beauty give you. Pair this environment with a pleasing scent, and some music … well, that thought just gave me chills.

This is a part of growing to One that you have probably already stumbled upon. Ones crave order, organization, and spaces that make sense. Not all Ones are necessarily clean; it may look more like organized chaos, but they still know where everything is.

We may not naturally be as organized as Ones, but we thrive in the spaces they create. This very fact may have prompted you to become more organized. Congratulations—that is a sign of growth!

For the rest of us, our craft areas may not stay clean for long, but when they are, it's easier for us to get things done and to access the most creative parts of our minds. I know you may be nodding your head as you read this!

How do we purposefully utilize this fact about ourselves for our own growth and peace of mind? We act on this belief that we do better in organized and beautiful spaces by prioritizing both cleanliness and aesthetics. Start with one area that you see every day—your bedside table, bathroom, desk—whatever makes the most sense for you. You then get to implement some discipline, consistency, and action by *keeping* it clean.

I know this isn't a fun exercise, but to get you excited, give yourself an allowance for some new decor to complement the space you're organizing. You might be surprised how keeping an area organized and beautiful helps you think clearer, feel more peaceful, and foster even more action-oriented habits.

SHIFT IN FOCUS

As we touched on earlier, God cares about aesthetics. So much so that He gave clear instructions to those building His temple and tabernacle down to the color, design, and thread count of the curtains. God cares about beauty, but even more than that, He cares about your heart and what makes it do a little happy dance. He's a Father, and He likes to give good gifts to His children.

Spend some time thinking about both your last and next project where you, like God, get to design and implement beauty into your space.

• • • • • • • • • • • • DAY 59

The Healthy Four

But God shows his love for us in that while we were still sinners,
Christ died for us.
(Romans 5:8)

Your inner world will always be creative, you will never run out of awe when you stare at God's creation, and your heart will always be tender to the pain of others. None of the greatest parts of your Four-ness change from going to One. One-ness only enhances the best parts of being a Four.

A healthy Four not only dreams, but also acts on their dreams. They still feel envy, but they have disciplined themselves to push through the nagging urge to quit. They still feel the waves of emotion, but they can tap into more logical thinking as they sort through emotions. They still are tempted to emotionally spiral, but they know that unless they are willing to take action, they don't get to indulge in that emotional abyss.

We don't ever *become* a One, and going to One definitely won't give us an inner critic. You won't lose the best parts of your Four-ness that you love, but you will start to make more sense to yourself. You'll be able to pre-plan for events or situations that might cause you to envy or emotionally spiral, and let God help you. You'll push through *doing repression* and envy to get to action, and from there, you will start to change the world around you.

You'll be a Four who is proud of yourself, a Four who isn't a slave to how you feel, a Four who values what you add to the world. You will also see the unique value others add to you.

Once action and discipline become consistent, you'll have more room for logical processing of emotions, leading to responding instead of reacting, helping you to obey God and be proud of yourself in the process. Helping you love not only yourself but others the way that God loves, unconditionally. Always remember, God's love is unconditional, without ulterior motives, and it has no limits.

It's easier to spot Satan's lies when you believe that you're loved, and it's hard for him to tempt you with envy when you love others like you love yourself.

SHIFT IN FOCUS

Dear Heavenly Father, I thank You that what may feel so out of reach for me is possible with You. Help me to act, help me to grow in discipline, and logical processing of my emotions. I want to honor You with my actions and emotions. Please show me how this looks, and convict me of the actions and emotions I am currently indulging in that are not honoring to You. Thank You for loving me so much that You sent Your son to die for me. I do not, nor could I ever, deserve that sacrifice. Please help me to live like I am loved that much, and I thank You that I am. Amen.

• • • • • • • • • • • • DAY 60

The Four in Action

*Practice these things, immerse yourself in them,
so that all may see your progress.*
(1 Timothy 4:15)

Action, at first, may feel like jumping off a cliff. Every moment you are convicted to assert yourself, claim your space, and follow your dream may feel too costly to follow through on. Again and again, you may fail to take the jump because it just feels too scary, and then you'll feel beaten down and not enough yet again. This is the challenge of being motivated by peace, and this cycle is something Satan can use to make sure you never walk in the freedom of your worth in Christ.

Satan is all about stopping your growth from coming to fruition. I wouldn't be surprised if you even notice elements of spiritual attack as you prioritize growth, but that doesn't mean the growth isn't God's heart for you.

Even if you get discouraged when Going to One in growth, remember that life is seasonal. You cannot achieve your *ideal growth* because you will never be without a sin nature while you're here on Earth. However, this doesn't mean that you are not still growing; by the power of the Holy Spirit, you are in the beautiful process of becoming who God created you to be.

Don't let two steps forward and one step back discourage you. This is still moving forward; this is still growth.

Action may feel like jumping off a cliff because you're trusting God for the outcome. You're trusting that obedience is better than complacency. You're trusting that God meant it when He said He made you as an equal to everyone else. You're trusting, like the child at the edge of the pool jumping into their father's arms, that God is ready to catch you.

SHIFT IN FOCUS

Here, we are going to use 1 Timothy 4:15 as a guideline for action: *"Practice these things, immerse yourself in them, so that all may see your progress."*

"Practice these things…"

Every new thing you've ever done needed some practice. Growing in going to Three is no different. Practice asserting yourself, claiming your space, taking steps toward dreams, or growing in confidence. These may look like a dozen little steps, small victories that maybe only you and God notice. Don't be afraid to be in the mindset of practice.

"…immerse yourself in them…"

Which verse that we mentioned over the last ten days really resonated with you? Memorize it, write it out, and place it somewhere you will see it. Immerse yourself in the truth of your worth in Christ, and you'll find yourself slowly but surely believing it to be true.

"…so that all may see your progress."

Pick a couple of people in your life to share your big or small victories with. I hope you have people who come to mind right away. If not, there are plenty of Instagram or Facebook pages for Fours who would love to cheer you on in your Four-ish wins. Be bold and share them as something worth celebrating. Get yourself a coffee or have a bowl of ice cream. Life is hard, and any victories are worth celebrating with God and others. Thank you for letting me share part of this journey with you!

Book Recommendations for Fours

Jennie Allen, *Nothing to Prove: Why We Can Stop Trying so Hard* (Colorado Springs, CO: Waterbrook Publishing, 2018)

Lysa TerKeurst, *Uninvited: Living Loved When You Feel Less Than, Left Out, and Lonely* (Nashville, TN: Thomas Nelson, 2016)

Alia Joy, *Glorious Weakness: Discovering God in All We Lack* (Chicago, IL: Baker Books, 2019)

Elyse Fitzpatrick, *Good News for Weary Women: Escaping the Bondage of To-Do Lists, Steps, and Bad Advice* (Chicago, IL: Tyndale House Publishers, 2014)

K.J. Ramsey, *This Too Shall Last: Finding Grace When Suffering Lingers* (Grand Rapids, MI: Zondervan, 2020)

Rebecca K. Reynolds, *Courage, Dear Heart: Letters to a Weary World* (Colorado Springs, CO: NavPress, 2018)

Leanna Tankersley, *Begin Again: The Brave Practice of Releasing Hurt and Receiving Rest* (Ada, MI: Revell, 2018)

Emily P. Freeman, *A Million Little Ways: Uncover The Art You Were Made To Live* (Ada, MI: Revell, 2013)

Ann Voskamp, *One Thousand Gifts: A Dare to Live Fully Right Where You Are* (Grand Rapids, MI: Zondervan, 2011)

As the Enneagram has passed through many hands, and been taught by various wonderful people, I want to acknowledge that none of the concepts or ideas of the Enneagram have been created by me. I'd like to give thanks to the Enneagram teachers and pioneers who have gone before me, and whose work has influenced this devotional:

Suzanne Stabile

Ian Morgan Cron

Father Richard Rhor

Don Richard Riso

Russ Hudson

Beatrice Chestnut

Beth McCord

Ginger Lapid-Bogda

About the Author

Elisabeth Bennett first discovered the Enneagram in the summer of 2017 and immediately realized how life-changing this tool could be. She set out to absorb all she could about this ancient personality typology, including a twelve-week Enneagram Certification course taught by Beth McCord, who has studied the Enneagram for more than twenty-five years.

In 2018, Elisabeth started her own Enneagram Instagram account (@EnneagramLife), which has grown to nearly 65,000 followers. Since becoming a certified Enneagram coach, Elisabeth has conducted more than one hundred one-on-one coaching sessions to help her clients find their type and apply the Enneagram to their lives for personal and spiritual growth. She has also conducted staff/team building sessions for businesses and high school students.

Elisabeth has lived in beautiful Washington State her entire life and now has the joy of raising her own children there with her husband, Peter.

To contact Elisabeth, please visit:

www.elisabethbennettenneagram.com

www.instagram.com/enneagram.life